RECORDS OF BRIDPORT FRATERNITIES

# RECORDS OF BRIDPORT FRATERNITIES

## 1271 – 1530

*Edited by*

ANTONY WILSDON

DORSET RECORD SOCIETY

VOLUME 22

© Dorset Record Society 2022

Dorset Record Society
Dorset History Centre, Bridport Road, Dorchester, Dorset DT1 1XA

General Editor: Dr Mark Forrest

Typeset in ITC New Baskerville by John Chandler,

British Library Cataloguing in Publication Data:
A catalogue record for this book is available from the British Library.

ISBN 978-0-900339-25-7

# CONTENTS

*List of illustrations*     *vii*
*Acknowledgements*     *viii*

**Introduction**     *xi*
  Preliminary remarks     *xi*
  1. Mediaeval Bridport     *xii*
  2. Parish Fraternities (National)     xv
    *2.1 Terminology and origins*     *xv*
    *2.2 Popularity and spread in late mediaeval England*     *xvi*
    *2.3 Purpose of the fraternities*     *xvii*
    *2.4 Financing the fraternities*     *xix*
    *2.5 Documentary sources (national)*     *xx*
    *2.6 The Reformation and end of the fraternities*     *xxi*
  3. The Bridport Fraternities     *xxii*
    *3.1 Number and location of the fraternities*     *xxii*
    *3.2 Nature and content of documents*     *xxiii*
    *3.3 The Lists of members*     *xxiv*
    *3.4 The Ordinances*     *xxvi*
    *3.5 The Annual Meeting for Accounts and Election of Wardens*     *xxviii*
    *3.6 Financial records*     *xxx*
    *3.7 Title deeds*     *xxxi*
  4. The Bridport Fraternities – the Members     *xxxiii*
    *4.1 Gender*     *xxxiv*
    *4.2 Social status and Occupation*     *xxxv*
    *4.3 Multiple Membership*     *xxxvi*
    *4.4 Office Holders*     *xxxvii*
    *4.5 Individual lives*     *xxxviii*
  5. Description of the Documents     *xl*
    *5.1 Form and condition*     *xl*
    *5.2 Language*     *xli*
    *5.3 Handwriting*     *xliii*
    *5.4 Unrelated material within the documents*     *xliv*
  6. Editorial conventions     *xlv*

*Bibliography*     *xlvi*

**The texts**

Various fraternities, fundraising accounts, 1454-1458     1
The Fraternity of the Light Hanging before the Cross, 1425-1461
    Volume containing membership list, ordinances, elections and accounts     3
Fraternity of the Mortuary Lights in St Mary's, 1333-1342
    Title deed, 1333     11
    Title deed, 1342     12
Fraternity of St Nicholas, 1423-1437
    Volume containing membership list, ordinances, elections and accounts     12
Fraternity of the Torches, 1425-1461
    Volume containing membership list, elections and accounts     18
Fraternity of the Two Torches, 1419-1480
    Volume containing membership list, ordinances, elections and accounts     32
Fraternity of St Katherine
    Volume containing membership list, ordinances, elections and accounts     42
    Title deeds, 1359-1493     49
Fraternity of the Blessed Virgin Mary, 1462-1530
    Accounts     55
    Title deeds     64
Fraternity of the Holy Cross in the chapel of St Andrew, 1470
    Accounts     67
Fraternity of the Holy Trinity, 1271-1280
    Title deeds     68
Fraternity of St Mary and St James, 1406-1464
    Volume containing membership list, ordinances, elections and accounts     72

**Appendix A**
Wainwright's transcription of the lost volume containing the membership list, accounts and ordinances of the Fraternity of the Light of the Holy Cross     78

**Appendix B**
Reprint of section from Historical Manuscripts Commission report relating to the lost volume of the Fraternity of the Light of the Holy Cross     87

**Appendix C**
Section from the Customary of Sarum used as a binding     88

*Index*     93

# LIST OF ILLUSTRATIONS

Map of Bridport showing key locations circa 1450. *ix*

Plan of the Church of St Mary, Bridport. *x*

DC-BTB/CD/6/1, Monies received and expenses incurred by William Oliver. *xx*

DC-BTB/CD/56, List of members of the Fraternity of St Mary and St James. *xxv*

DC-BTB/CD/56, Ordinances of the Fraternity of St Mary and St James. *xxvii*

DC-BTB/CD/12b, Title deed: lease by the wardens of the Fraternity of the
Mortuary Lights of land in South Street, 1333. *xxxii*

DC-BTB/CD/15, Part of a sermon in English at the end of a volume of
annual accounts relating to the Fraternity of St Nicholas. *xlii*

The first page of DC-BTB/CD11. Members of the Fraternity of the Light
Hanging before the Cross. 2

The first page of DC-BTB/CD/14 names of the members of the
Fraternity of St Nicholas. 13

Outer front cover, DC-BTB/CD/15, mediaeval music. 19

Inner front cover, DC-BTB/CD/15, mediaeval music. 20

Outer back cover, DC-BTB/CD/15, mediaeval music. 30

Inner back cover, DC-BTB/CD/15, mediaeval music. 31

The first page of DC-BTB/CD/22 names of the members of the
Fraternity of St Katherine. 41

DC-BTB/CD/33, Receipts of the Fraternity of Our Lady, circa 1475. 63

DC-BTB/PQ/28, Wainwright's transcription of the lost book of the Fraternity
of the Light of the Holy Cross. 87

DC-BTB/CD/11, Section of the customary of Sarum recycled as book binding. 92

*Front cover image*, DC-BTB/CD/56, see p. xxv.

*Back cover image*, The cover and first page of DC-BTB/CD/11, see p. 2 (the cover is a
page from a recycled Customary of Sarum, see p. 90).

## ACKNOWLEDGEMENTS

The editor would particularly like to thank Mark Forrest , for initially recruiting him as a volunteer at Dorset History Centre, for introducing him to the fascinating world of mediaeval records, for helping him to acquire the skills needed to read the documents, and for his patient support and assistance in the preparation of this volume.

**Antony Wilsdon** began to volunteer at Dorset History Centre in 2012, after retiring from a career in local government. His background as a linguist led him to work chiefly on the cataloguing and calendaring of documents in Latin and Norman French. This in turn required him to acquire a knowledge of paleography and to develop a greater understanding of the historical background to these documents, most of which dated to the centuries preceding the Reformation. Living near Bridport, he relished the opportunity to translate the Fraternity records which form the subject of this book.

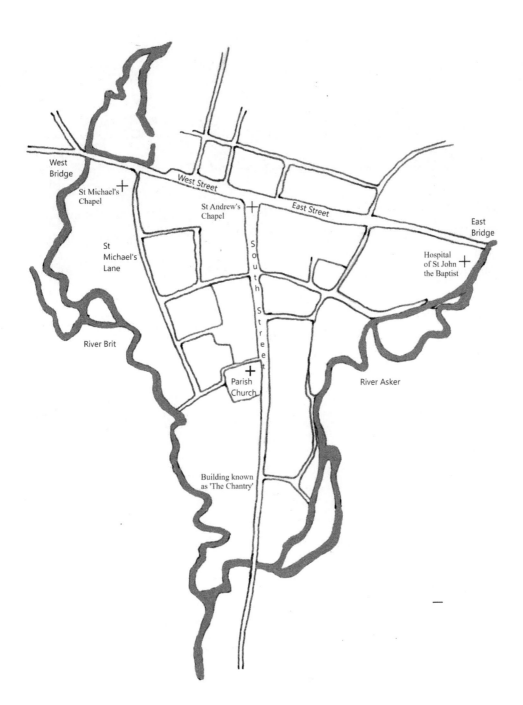

West
Bridge

West Street

St Michael's
Chapel

St Andrew's
Chapel

East Street

East
Bridge

St
Michael's
Lane

South Street

Hospital
of St John
the Baptist

River Brit

River Asker

Parish
Church

Building known
as 'The Chantry'

*Bridport circa 1450, after Penn, Historic Towns of Dorset.*

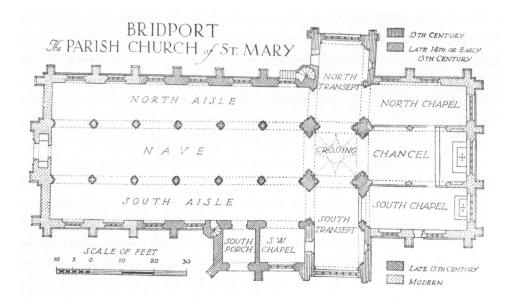

*Plan of the Church of St Mary, Bridport. Royal Commission on Historical Monuments,*
*West Dorset, page 44.*

# INTRODUCTION

**Preliminary remarks**

This book contains transcriptions and translations of documents relating to the parish fraternities of Bridport during the later Middle Ages. The story of these bodies, which played an important part in the life of towns all over England for several hundred years, is relatively unknown today to the general public. This volume will shed some light on this aspect of our local history.

The documents form part of the Bridport Borough Archive held at the Dorset History Centre. This impressive collection consists of over a thousand items, dating from the thirteenth to the twentieth century. The documents contained in the archive relate to a wide range of activities, including law enforcement, the administration of justice, local government, religious life, trade and industry and the buying and selling of land and houses. Bridport is indeed fortunate that such a rich source of historical material has survived and is available to those studying the past of this interesting town.

Within the borough archive are a considerable number of manuscripts relating to the late mediaeval period. These have the potential to illuminate the life of the town in the centuries before the Reformation. However they are written almost entirely in Latin and in a handwriting that is difficult for the unpractised reader (even one who has some knowledge of Latin) to decipher.

Two publications have sought to remedy this situation. In 1877 the Royal Commission on Historical Manuscripts included, in the Appendix to their 6th Report, a description of a large number of mediaeval documents from the "Records of the Bridport Corporation", a few of them translated in full. In 1900 Thomas Wainwright, an antiquarian from Barnstaple, published *The Bridport Borough Records and Ancient Manuscripts*, reproducing a series of articles originally written for the Bridport News. In this publication, long out of print, Wainwright offers a translation of a number of manuscripts.

Some of the records relating to the subject of this present volume, the *Records of Bridport Fraternities, 1271-1530*, are among those described or translated in these two publications. However it cannot be said that access to either of them is particularly easy (although both can be consulted at the Dorset History Centre, and although a determined searcher can hunt down Royal Commission on Historical Manuscripts publications on-line). The purpose of this volume is therefore to provide an easy route for interested readers to access this material, by bringing together and translating into English all the surviving manuscripts produced by the fraternities of Bridport.

Before presenting the translated text, it is necessary to provide some background to the documents in question. This will be done, in the remainder of this Introduction, as follows:

Section 1 briefly summarises the history of mediaeval Bridport. The town of this period would not be totally unfamiliar, in terms of its geography, to a modern inhabitant. The basic "T-shape" created by the junction of South Street with East and West Streets has remained the same. The parish church occupies the same site.

Section 2 looks at the phenomenon of parish fraternities in England, touching on their pre-Conquest origins but focusing mainly on their popularity and spread in the centuries before the Reformation. This section addresses the deceptively simple question "What were they for?" before discussing how they were financed. After a brief look at the documentary sources available at a national level, it describes how the fraternities, like the monasteries and the chantries, came to an end in the 16th century with the religious reforms of Henry VIII and Edward VI.

Section 3 focuses on the Bridport fraternities, naming the ten bodies for whom records survive and describing the nature and contents of the chosen documents. These documents give us an insight into how these bodies organised themselves, how they sought to fulfil their primary objectives, how they provided benefits to their membership, and how they financed their activities.

Section 4 will explore what can be gleaned from the records about the 612 individuals who are mentioned in them as members of one or more of the ten fraternities. Questions of gender and social status will be touched upon, as will the characteristics of those holding particular fraternity offices. The occurrence within the fraternity membership of members of the clergy and of people holding wider borough offices will be commented on. Finally some individual fraternity members who emerge from the mass of names will be highlighted. These are individuals whose names occur in other contemporary records, allowing a rare glimpse into their lives outside their involvement in the fraternity movement, including, for example, office holding in other lay or religious institutions.

Section 5 describes the documents themselves in terms of their physical form, their condition and the language in which they are written.

Finally Section 6 sets out the editorial decisions that have shaped this current volume.

## 1. Mediaeval Bridport

The town of Bridport had existed since at least the 9th century, when it was developed by King Alfred as part of the defence of the coast against Danish invaders.[1] The Domesday survey of 1086 records that at that time Bridport was a town of 100 houses. In 1150 Henry Plantagenet (later to rule England as Henry II) took Bridport by storm during his campaign against King Stephen. The submission of Bridport's castellan is mentioned, implying that a castle existed at this time, but its whereabouts are unknown.[2]

In 1213 King John, at war with France, ordered that ropes should be made at Bridport for his ships. It is possible that King John became familiar with the town and

1    Penn, *Historic Towns of Dorset*, p. 23
2    Hindson, Bridport: Burgh and Borough, p. 10

its trade during his several visits to his hunting lodge at Powerstock.[3]

In 1253 Henry III granted a charter to his royal borough of Bridport.[4] This key event in the town's history took place just eighteen years before the earliest date occurring in the records of the Bridport fraternities. The 1253 Charter conferred certain important liberties on the burgesses of the town. These were the freemen (estimated at about a third of the population) who held land by burgage tenure with its attendant rights and responsibilities. The charter confirmed their freedom from various feudal dues and their right to a certain level of self-government through the annual election of two bailiffs from their number. The bailiffs were responsible for paying to the King his agreed "farm" - the annual sum of money paid by the royal boroughs to the Exchequer. Throughout the period covered by the fraternity records, the bailiffs can be seen to play a leading role in the administration of Bridport's affairs.

Some levels of Bridport society are more visible than others in the surviving records of the borough. This is certainly true of the fraternity records where it seems likely that almost all the individuals named belong to the classes between the extremely poor and the wealthy aristocracy. But, hard though it is to build a picture of how the whole population lived, it can be said that Bridport was one of a small number of Dorset towns with an urban centre and a manufacturing sector that differentiated it from the surrounding rural economy. A Jewish community was present by 1265.[5]

The thirteenth century had been good to Bridport, as indeed to many towns across England. The town became more prosperous – no doubt Bridport's reputation for producing good quality ropes and yarns with hemp grown locally was an important factor. Prosperity led to an expansion of Bridport from the original Saxon town, which had been centred around the parish church in South Street. The area to the north of East and West Street (the old Roman road to Exeter) was developed and may have become known as the New Borough.[6] The 1253 Charter contained provision for an increase in the "farm" due to the King, in all likelihood reflecting the increase in population during the 13th century.

The current parish church of St Mary the Virgin was built in the early 13th century, though a Saxon church probably existed on the same site. It was built as a cruciform church in the Early English style.[7] Of this 13th century building, however, only the north and south transepts remain. A lengthy rebuilding campaign took place in the late 14th and early 15th centuries, during which the great central tower and a four bay aisled nave were completed in the Perpendicular style. This was a period in which such improvements to church buildings, in the latest gothic style, were happening across the country, financed by the laity. In rural areas funds were often provided by a wealthy lord, while in towns a corporation or a collection of parishioners might be responsible for raising the money needed.

Subsequent rebuilding in the Victorian period (led by the architect John Hicks) has meant that only one chapel has survived from the mediaeval building, the small

3    Hindson, *Bridport: Burgh and Borough*, p. 11
4    Barker, *The Bridport Charter of 1253*.
5    Penn, *Historic Towns of Dorset*, p.26
6    Penn, *Historic Towns of Dorset*, pp.23-9.
7    Royal Commission on Historical Monuments,, *West Dorset*, pp.43-5

south-west chapel adjacent to the south porch. This was dedicated to St Katherine and was the site of a chantry, founded in the 14th century.

By the middle of the 13th century it seems that the expansion of the population to the north of the town prompted the building of a new church, dedicated to St Andrew, located at the site of the current Town Hall at the top of South Street. This was intended to serve the needs of the new town. It never became a parish church however – the rectors of St Mary's actively opposed any such development and ensured that it remained a chapel under their authority. No trace of this building remains.

Other religious establishments included the Hospital of St John the Baptist by the east bridge, which provided lodgings for travellers arriving in the town, and the leper hospital of St Mary Magdalene just over the then borough boundary in Allington to the west. A chapel dedicated to St Michael existed from at least the 13th century and was the site of a chantry founded by a prominent inhabitant of Bridport, John Munden, in 1361. Here two chaplains were maintained to celebrate daily masses on behalf of the benefactor and other named souls. The day-to-day life of these chantry priests has been illuminated in Katherine Wood-Legh's transcription of the Munden's Chantry account book, *A Small Household of the Fifteenth Century*. The building known as "The Chantry" in South Street, and formerly thought to be a possible location for Munden's Chantry, is now thought to have been a merchant's house.

The arrival of the bubonic plague (the "Black Death") in 1348 and subsequent years is often cited as a reason for the decline in prosperity which affected towns like Bridport in the 14th century. There is no doubt that Bridport was heavily hit by the outbreak of the disease. Four bailiffs are named as having held office during the year 1349/50 which is named in the records as "the Year of Pestilence" – it seems that only one, Richard Laurens, survived.[8] A rector of St Mary's also perished in this year. But it has been demonstrated, by reference to tax records and other sources, that the town had been in economic decline since at least the second decade of the 14th century, as the town lost out to the growing towns of Lyme Regis, Melcombe Regis and Weymouth, all of which had better harbours.[9] If Bridport did indeed enjoy a "Golden Age" during the 13th century, it was well and truly over even before the Black Death struck.

There are some indications of a recovery in the economic situation of Bridport during the late 14th and early 15th centuries, but it does not appear that Bridport was a truly prosperous place. In the mid fifteenth century the Bridport burgesses attempted to develop the town's harbour to compete with those at Lyme Regis, Weymouth and Melcombe Regis, which were benefiting from cross channel trade. In 1446 the Bailiffs applied to the Church for assistance in carrying out the improvements needed. The Bishop of Bath and Wells and other religious authorities issued indulgences, granting remission from Purgatory for all who piously contributed to the harbour works, stating that "the inhabitants of the said town of Bridport... are by no means able to make anew, repair and maintain the said harbour, unless help is mercifully given them

---

8     Dorset History Centre, DC-BTB/G/1.
9     Forrest, 'Dorset's trade networks', p.43.

in this matter by the pious alms of the faithful in Christ."[10] This project was ultimately unsuccessful and Bridport's harbour only ever engaged in trade along the English coast. Early in the 16th century, Bridport was among several "decayed towns upon which Henry VIII urged the necessity of effecting restorations".[11] .

However, although Bridport did not have continental trade its industrial sector was significant and the town had a well developed trade network. The rope-making industry continued to be of crucial importance to Bridport. In a battle against local competition the burgesses successfully petitioned Henry VIII for legislation forbidding anyone living within a five-mile radius of the town from selling hemp other than in the market at Bridport, and from making rope for sale.

Coming to a clear view of the prosperity or otherwise of Bridport at this period from existing records is difficult. It is interesting to note that when John Leland, commissioned by King Henry VIII to conduct a survey of England, came to Bridport in 1542, he described it as "a fine, large town".[12]

Nor do the records provide a picture of how the inhabitants of Bridport felt about the religious upheavals that began with reign of Henry VIII and his break with Rome. The Dorset monasteries,  the Hospital of St John the Baptist, the Allington leper hospital, the chantries and the parish fraternities all disappeared within a short space of time from the lives of the people of the town. It is hard to imagine that these changes occurred without stirring up strong feelings in many people. At a national level the reactions of ordinary people to these dramatic events and the ongoing religious changes can be seen in periodic "commotions" such as the Prayer Book Rebellion in Devon and Cornwall – but the feelings of the people of Bridport have left no trace.

## 2   Parish Fraternities - National

### 2.1 Terminology and origins

The bodies which are the subject of this book used the Latin word "fraternitas" (or sometimes "confraternitas") to describe themselves, meaning "brotherhood". In the English speaking world today the word "fraternity" is perhaps most often used in connection with certain student societies in the United States. In Catholic Europe, however,  this word is still frequently used to refer to very much the same phenomenon as witnessed in mediaeval Bridport - bodies of lay people who come together for religious (and social) purposes.  In the cities of Spain during Holy Week, for example, huge sculptures depicting the Easter story are carried around the streets by the members of various local brotherhoods, known as "cofradías", a Spanish form of "confraternitates". Each one of these brotherhoods (there are seventy in the Seville processions alone) is responsible for its part of the procession and for looking after their image during the year.

This type of religious fraternity has a long history, dating back in England to well before the Norman Conquest. Records exist, for example, of a fraternity at

10    Dorset History Centre, DC-BTB/N/4-9.
11    Victoria County History , Vol.2, p.246
12    Chandler, *Leyland's Itinerary*, p.132.

Abbotsbury in the tenth century.[13] The very early fraternities had close links with neighbouring monasteries - the members of the Abbotsbury fraternity were required to contribute regularly to the maintenance of the Abbey of St Peter. But there are striking similarities to be observed in comparing the rules governing this Anglo-Saxon fraternity with those of the later mediaeval period, demonstrating the notable continuity of the tradition.

The Old English word generally used for these bodies in the tenth century was "gild", and some historians have favoured this term (either spelled in this way or as "guild") to describe the brotherhoods throughout the middle ages. However, because the word "guild" has become associated particularly with trade or craft guilds (in which sense it continues to be used today) we will use the word "fraternity" for the parish-based bodies under discussion. It needs to be said in passing, though, that it is a mistake to make too rigid a distinction between "religious" fraternities and "secular" trade or craft guilds – the latter bodies would not have understood that distinction, having themselves many aims that we might nowadays describe as "religious".[14]

*2.2 Popularity and spread in late mediaeval England*

From the late fourteenth century onwards there was a remarkable proliferation of these parish fraternities. The historian Eamon Duffy suggests that in the late mediaeval period many towns of England "harboured literally dozens of them".[15] Kings Lynn, for example, is known to have had over seventy fraternities, Bodmin over forty. As we shall see, even a town like Bridport is known to have had more than ten. Later this spread into the more rural areas with the result, according to Duffy, that by the time of England's break with Rome most villages had at least one such fraternity. What lay behind the growing popularity of this movement?

The national trauma of the Black Death undoubtedly had a significant impact on the way many people in England viewed their lives. It is easy to imagine how the experience of seeing friends and family snatched away without warning by the plague would lead people to reflect on their own mortality and to place a high value on any activity promising to ensure a better outcome for themselves in the afterlife.

While there was an increase in more individual, personal forms of religion during the period after the Black Death, it is certainly not the case that public and indeed corporate forms of religion became less important. As Rosser argues persuasively in his book *The Art of Solidarity in the Middle Ages*, individualism and communal feeling were not necessarily in conflict.[16] The foundation of so many parish fraternities across the country in the late fourteenth century may reflect a wish by many to replace the family structures that had been destroyed by the plague. An aspect of this may well have been a wish, on the part of those joining fraternities, to ensure that there were people around who would ensure that they would receive a proper funeral when they died.

---

13    Whitlock, 'Abbotsbury Guild Statutes', in *English Historical Documents*, pp.660-3.
14    Brown, *Popular Piety*, p.148.
15    Duffy, *Stripping of the Altars*, p.142.
16    Rosser, *Art of Solidarity*, pp. 13-17

## 2.3 Purposes of the fraternities

Before discussing in more detail the principal functions of the fraternities, it is important to consider the relationship of these bodies with the existing parish organisation, as embodied in the rector and the churchwardens. There is evidence to support the view that traditional parishes, somewhat inflexible in their structures, were becoming less able to meet all the changing needs of their parishioners. In a society slowly becoming more mobile the fact that a parish organisation served only those living within a strictly defined geographical area may have been a factor. Parish membership was automatically conferred by residence, but fraternity membership was voluntary, and could cut across parish boundaries, allowing those living in different parishes with shared devotional aims or a shared desire for social contacts to meet together.

However there is much evidence to show that the fraternities were not generally in conflict or in competition with the parish authorities. On the contrary they frequently worked with the rector and the churchwardens to enhance the worship of the parish church. Being a member of a parish fraternity was, in the words of Duffy, "more often than not simply one of the conventional ways of being an active parishioner".[17] This may have been particularly true in a town like Bridport where the parish of St Mary the Virgin served the whole borough.

The three principal functions of fraternities were i) the maintenance of lights within a parish church or a chapel; ii) the spiritual well-being of its members, achieved by intercessions for the living and the dead and by ensuring suitable funerals and iii) the provision of social benefits, including the relief of distress when members fell on hard times.

"Lights" or candles were of great importance in late mediaeval churches, which typically contained a large number, some kept permanently alight, some lit for special occasions. The great Cross or Rood which hung at the junction of the nave and the chancel was supported on a "rood loft" or "candle beam" where lights could be maintained. Around the church, in chapels and side aisles, niches would contain images of saints to be honoured by the lighting of a candle. More lights would be lit at seasons such as Easter, or at funerals.

Someone needed to look after all these candles, ensuring that adequate stocks of wax were maintained and that the lights were tended as they should be. Arrangements for this varied across the country and between parishes. Parish fraternities played a vital role in many churches, maintaining the lights before the images of their various patron saints.

Alongside the maintenance of lights, the fraternities aimed to provide spiritual benefits to their members by ensuring that their souls would be regularly prayed for during life and, especially, after death. It was a characteristic belief of late mediaeval Christians that the period spent by a soul in purgatory could be shortened and alleviated by the intercession of the living and especially by the holding of masses for the dead. Joining a parish fraternity, with a modest entry fee and a manageable annual contribution, was an affordable way of achieving this aim. A distinction existed

17    Duffy, *Stripping of the Altars*, p. 154

between wealthier fraternities who could actually employ their own chaplain, and others who would provide lights on altars and only pay a priest when needed to conduct masses for the souls of deceased members.

A closely related preoccupation was the desire to have a decent funeral at which the prayers of the faithful and the holding of a special mass would ease one's parting from life. An almost universal feature of the rules or "ordinances" which members of every fraternity swore to obey was a requirement for every member to attend the requiem mass for a deceased fellow member. Failure to attend without reasonable excuse would lead to a fine.

The possibility of losing one's life away from home and being buried in a strange place was a troubling one. Fraternities frequently made provision for this in their ordinances, with a view to ensuring that the body of any member who died within a specified distance of the parish would be brought back and suitably buried.

It would be misleading to draw a rigid distinction between the "religious" and the "social" functions of the parish fraternities. Nonetheless it is clear that among the motivations of those joining these bodies are some that we would see as primarily social.

On the feast day of their patron saint, after a procession and a mass in the parish church, most if not all parish fraternities celebrated with a special feast. From innumerable records and accounts of fraternities across England the importance of this annual event is obvious.

Aside from the holding of a great annual feast, the raising of money by selling ale was a commonplace. In some parishes such "church ales" were a major source of funding for the church.

Rosser sees the construction of social networks as a central aspect of parish fraternities, describing the voluntary act of joining a fraternity as making a commitment to a community of friends. Here it is relevant to mention the fact that virtually all fraternities admitted men and women as equal members, providing, in Rosser's words "an irreproachable context within which to socialise and build relationships".[18]

Such social networking may often have involved a wish to maintain or improve one's social standing. Being a member of any fraternity probably conferred some sort of social credit – they would have been seen as morally positive organisations. But it is clear that some fraternities were more prestigious than others, with some drawing their membership from the upper levels of their town's society, as can sometimes be seen by comparison with lists of those holding prestigious municipal offices.

In general it can be said that the fraternities took their members from a fairly wide cross-section of the community – but that the very poorest would probably have been excluded, as being unable to afford the required entrance fees and annual subscriptions, and equally unable to purchase the respectable clothing that would have been expected at fraternity gatherings.

Provision was made, however, within the ordinances of most fraternities in England, for the financial support of members who fell on hard times. The following from the Guild of St Mary, Beverley, is typical: "The Alderman and Stewards of the gild shall visit those bretheren and sisteren who are poor, ailing, or weak, and who have

18  Rosser, *Art of Solidarity*, p.111

not enough of their own to live upon: and they shall give to these as they think right out of the gild stock, as has been agreed; namely, to each one being so poor, ailing, or weak, eighteen pence, sixpence or at least fourpence, every week, to help their needs".[19] However charity directed to the poor who were not fraternity members, though it does occur, seems to have been less common. When such wider relief of poverty was included in the rules of a fraternity, a distinction between the deserving and undeserving poor would generally be made.

## *2.4 Financing the fraternities*

The surviving records of the fraternities across the country provide a somewhat patchy picture of how they were financed. Particular accounts can appear to be reasonably detailed, but often omit, frustratingly, certain key elements, leaving many unanswered questions.

The fraternities obtained their income from a number of different sources. These included:

- Bequests from deceased members and other well-wishers, sometimes in the form of money, sometimes in the form of household items or livestock which could be sold for cash.
- Entrance fees (often 6s 8d) and a fairly modest annual subscription, often just a few pence. Membership of a fraternity was probably affordable to all but the very poor.
- Fines, in money or in kind, payable by members who failed to adhere to the ordinances of the fraternity.
- Rental income from land and properties (some left to them in bequests, some leased as a business venture and sub-let).
- Fundraising efforts such as the holding of "ales".

The fraternities spent this money on:

- The purchasing of wax and wicks for the candles and the funding of other activities connected with the honouring of images in the church.
- Paying priests to conduct occasional funerals and special masses (paying the salary of a full-time priest would be beyond the reach of all but the wealthiest fraternities).
- Purchasing food and drink for the annual fraternity feast, often a lavish affair, with no expense spared. Farnhill lists the purchases made by the Fraternity of St George in Wymondham, Norfolk, in preparation for their feast: two calves, six sheep, eight pigs and twenty six geese, amounting to a grand total of £3 15s 1½d.[20] In addition to the food and drink there was often the expense of hiring a hall and engaging minstrels for the entertainment of the feasting brothers and sisters.
- The charitable activities of the fraternities, whether directed exclusively to their own members who had fallen on hard times or (more rarely) to the wider population of the poor.

19   Toulmin Smith, *English Gilds*, p.150.
20   Farnhill, *Guilds and the Parish Community*, p.78.

- Meeting expenses connected with the fraternities' ownership of land and properties, such as the maintenance of houses let to tenants.

As stated at the beginning of this section, obtaining a full and accurate picture of any particular fraternity's financial position from the surviving accounts is not generally possible. However the foregoing can serve as a broad summary of the main items of income and expenditure that can be discerned from the fraternity records across the country.

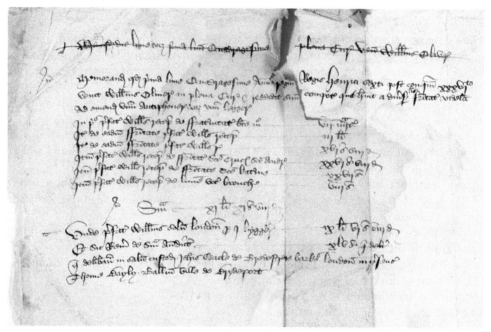

*DC-BTB/CD/6/1: monies received and expenses incurred by William Oliver.*

### 2.5 Documentary sources (national)

Our knowledge of parish fraternities at a national level has been increased by the study of returns from two particular government surveys. The first of these took place at the end of the fourteenth century and the second during the final days of the fraternities in the reign of Edward VI.

In 1389 the wardens of all fraternities in England were required by the government of Richard II to complete a return providing information about the way they were organised, their feasts and meetings, their ownership of land, buildings or goods and their charitable activities.[21] A comparison of the surviving returns with the list of known fraternities in any particular area, however, reveals that only a fraction are represented. In the whole of Dorset the only fraternity listed in the 1389 returns is the Guild of the Blessed Virgin Mary in Swanage. This is not untypical of many counties. It is not known whether the shortage of returns is simply because many have

---

21    Surviving certificates are held in the Chancery class C47 at the National Archives.

been lost, or whether fraternities refused to cooperate, believing, perhaps with some justification, that the purpose of the survey was to enable future taxation of their assets.

In 1548 the government of the boy king Edward VI instituted an enquiry to establish the endowed wealth of any remaining colleges, chantries, hospitals and fraternities which had survived earlier reforms. By this date it is possible that many fraternities had already been dissolved, along with the monasteries.

The returns from this survey, known as Chantry Certificates, are patchy, possibly as a result of widespread evasion. For the whole of Dorset, among the list of chantries and other institutions such as hospitals and free chapels, only five fraternities are recorded, one in each of the towns of Dorchester, Weymouth, Poole, Gillingham and Bridport.[22] The Bridport fraternity represented is that of the Blessed Mary in the parish church. Other Bridport institutions recorded in the Chantry Certificates are John Munden's Chantry, St Katherine's Chantry in the parish church and the Hospital of St John the Baptist. The Leper Hospital of St Mary Magdalen and a St Mary Magdalen's Chantry, both in Allington just outside the borough boundary, are also recorded.

### 2.6 The Reformation – end of the fraternities

While the final abolition of fraternities in England did not come until 1548, the process of dismantling the institutions of late mediaeval Catholic England began when, in 1534, through the Act of Supremacy, Henry VIII broke with Rome and styled himself Head of the Church in England. Between 1535 and 1540 the monasteries were dissolved, first the smaller houses and later the great monastic houses. The Chantries Act of 1545 conveyed to the Crown the property of all "colleges, free chapels, chantries, hospitals, fraternities, brotherhoods, gilds and stipendiary priests". During this period various religious practices were outlawed. Edward VI's government ordered the destruction of all images of saints in churches and outlawed the use of candles except in front of the sacrament. Throughout all this tumultuous period the doctrine of Purgatory and belief in the efficacy of masses for the dead, central to the raison d'être of the parish fraternities, came under sustained attack from the authorities and from the preachers of reform.

We simply do not know the state of the fraternities in Bridport nor the feelings of their members during this time of upheaval. It seems quite possible that Westlake's description of this confusing period would have rung true for many: "Verily men knew not what to believe, for the teaching of the clergy was as conflicting as the claims of the pamphleteers..".[23] But whatever the state of mind of the brethren and sisters of the parish fraternities, the final end arrived with the Chantries Act of 1548, which formally abolished the fraternities and brought to an end the long story of these bodies in England.

22   Fry, 'Dorset Chantries'.
23   Westlake, *Parish Guilds*, p.130.

## 3 The Bridport Fraternities

The proliferation of parish fraternities in the towns of late mediaeval England has already been referred to (2.2), and Bridport had a number of these bodies within its Borough area. The records of these institutions, preserved in the Bridport Borough Collection, are fragmentary, but represent the best set of fraternity documents for any town in Dorset.

### 3.1 Number and location of the fraternities

Records of ten fraternities have survived, all but three of which were located in the Parish Church of St Mary. The exceptions were the Fraternities of the Holy Cross, the Holy Trinity and St. Mary & St.James, all of which related to the Chapel of St Andrew, situated at the junction of South Street with East Street and West Street. As well as these ten fraternities references can be found to three or four others known only by their name.

The first document translated in this volume, DC-BTB/CD/6, is unique in not relating to a single fraternity but rather to an account of a fund-raising effort across several fraternities of the town. Among those listed is "The Fraternitas of St Thomas", the only evidence that such a body existed. In the same list is a reference to "The Light called Branch" as being another body donating money to the common cause (the purchase of "antiphoners" for the parish church), but the exact nature of this body is unknown.

The front cover of DC-BTB/CD/11 (which contains the records of the Fraternity of the Light Hanging before the Cross) is a parchment that has been "recycled" from a previous use. It consists of a fragment of a will, much of it barely legible, but which includes a legacy "to the Fraternity of St Swithin" – a tantalising glimpse of another fraternity which has left no other trace. Whether this fraternity related to St Mary's church in Bridport (to which another legacy is made) or whether it was connected with the parish church of Allington, just outside the town boundary, which was dedicated to St Swithin, is unknown.

Another glimpse of a "lost" fraternity is to be found in a document described in the Historical Manuscripts Commission (H.M.C.) (p.493) as "a paper account, in Latin, headed 'Payments by the hands of John Crosse in the fifth year of Henry the Sixth'". Among items in this document there is the following: "Paid the Clerk of the Fraternity of St John 12d".[24] It is possible that this fraternity was linked to the Hospital of St John the Baptist which was situated by the Asker bridge at the eastern approach to the town.

At this point it is worth addressing the fact that two of the fraternities (both, it seems, based at St. Mary's) had confusingly similar names. The records catalogued as DC-BTB/CD/15 relate to "the Fraternity of the Torches" (Fraternitas Torticiorum), while those of DC-BTB/CD/16 relate to "The Fraternity of the Two Candles, known as Torches)" (Fraternitas de duobus cereis quae vocatur Torchys). Both operated during the mid fifteenth century. Any suspicion that these were one and the same fraternity, however, is quickly dispelled by examination of the records. "Torches" held

---

24    H.M.C., *sixth report*, 493.

their annual meeting consistently on Palm Sunday, while "Two Torches" almost always met on the Tuesday after Easter. "Torches" appointed up to six wardens annually, "Two Torches" never more than three. Finally the membership lists show that, out of 120 named individuals associated with "Torches" and 124 associated with "Two Torches", only 14 people were members of both fraternities. The names of these fraternities reflect the fact that saints, who were seen as helpers more than as models of a virtuous life, were thought to value the lighting of candles before their image. No doubt the fact that this was a relatively cheap form of expressing devotion contributed to its popularity.

### 3.2 Nature and contents of documents

We turn to the Bridport records themselves and to the consideration of what has and what has not been preserved from the records of the ten parish fraternities discussed here. A total of 27 separately catalogued items within the Bridport Borough Collection held at the Dorset History Centre have been translated for the purpose of this book. (It should be noted that the Bridport Borough Collection also includes records of chantries, hospitals and other religious institutions of the mediaeval period, which are not included in the present volume). The following table summarises the contents of each of these 27 items:

| Catalogue Item / Document | Fraternity | Date range | Member lists | Ordinances (Rules of Fraternity) | Record of Annual Meetings | Accounts other than Annual Meeting | Title deeds |
|---|---|---|---|---|---|---|---|
| CD6 | Various | 1454 | | | | Record of fundraising for book purchase | |
| CD11 | Light hanging before the Cross | 1425-1461 | yes | yes | yes | | |
| CD12-13 | Mortuary Lights | 1333-1342 | | | | | yes |
| CD14 | St Nicholas | 1442-1437 | yes | yes | yes | | |
| CD15 | Torches | 1421-1458 | yes | Fragment only | yes | | |
| CD16 | Two Torches | 1419-1480 | yes | Fragment only | yes | yes | |
| CD22-27 | St. Katherine | 1356-1493 | yes | | yes | | yes |

| | | | | | | | |
|---|---|---|---|---|---|---|---|
| CD31 - 37 | Blessed Virgin Mary | 1443-1528 | yes (lists recording payment of Mass Penny ) | | | yes | yes |
| CD50 | Holy Cross | 1470 | | | yes | | |
| Wainwright Trans-cription | Holy Cross | 1399-1487 | yes | yes | yes | | |
| CD51 - 55 | Holy Trinity | 1271 | | | | | yes |
| CD56 | St. Mary & St. James | 1406-1454 | yes | yes | yes | | |

It can be seen from the above that the records of the Fraternity of the Holy Cross in the document CD/50 are limited to the record of annual meetings. In the course of preparing this volume it was noticed that the report of the Historical Manuscripts Commission (H.M.C.) seemed to refer to membership lists and other details of the Holy Cross Fraternity that were not present in CD/50. Further investigation revealed that the working papers of the Victorian antiquarian Thomas Wainwright have been deposited at the History Centre and that within these papers exists his handwritten translation of a further document relating to this particular fraternity. It is clear that the document in question was available both to the compiler of the H.M.C. report and to Thomas Wainwright, but has subsequently been lost. Wainwright's translation of these now lost records was not included in his publication of *The Bridport Borough Records and Ancient Manuscripts* in 1900, so the handwritten version within his papers remains the only evidence of their contents. For the sake of completeness Wainwright's translation of the Holy Cross records, lost prior to the deposit of the Bridport Borough Collection at the Dorset History Centre, has been included alongside the translation of CD/50.

*3.3 The Lists of Members*

It was of great importance to the fraternities to keep accurate membership lists, and these have survived in various degrees of completeness for seven of these bodies. Taken together they provide the names of more than 600 individuals involved in the Bridport fraternities between 1271 and 1528. Many of these individuals belonged to more than one fraternity (see 4.3 below). It is fascinating to see how many of the surnames are familiar to us today. The range of Christian names too is of some interest. Almost exactly a third of the named men were called John (122 out of 364). Second in popularity for males came William, 80 individuals having this name. Nearly a quarter of the named women were called Joan (57 out of 248) with Alice next in popularity (44 occurrences). There is not a single example of the name Mary in the membership lists, despite (or perhaps because of?) the widespread veneration of the Virgin. The name was becoming increasingly popular elsewhere in England so this may be evidence of local conservatism in the naming of children.

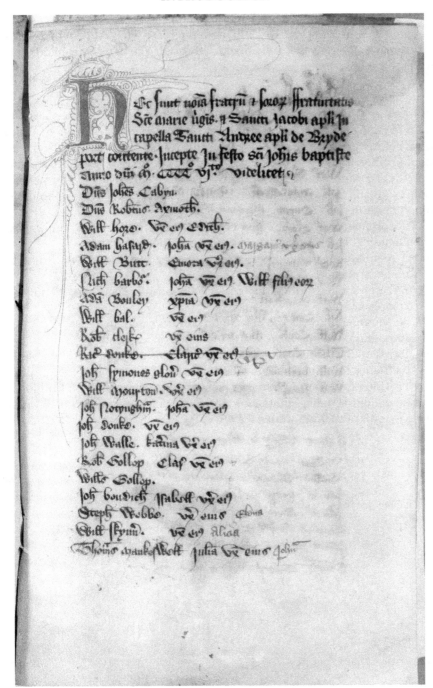

*DC-BTB/CD/56: list of members of the Fraternity of St Mary and St James.*

Unfortunately as a means of determining the numbers of fraternity members at any one time the surviving lists are difficult to interpret. They contain many crossings out which may well signify that a member is deceased. The same explanation may also apply to the symbol + beside some names.

## 3.4 The Ordinances

The "ordinances" or rules which the brothers and sisters agreed to obey have survived in an apparently complete form for four of the ten fraternities, namely: The Light Hanging before the Cross; St Nicholas; The Holy Cross; and St Mary & St James. The ordinances of the Fraternity of the Two Torches have survived in a more fragmentary form. In the accounts of the Fraternity of the Torches there is a single reference to the ordinances (as an explanation of a fee levied on members for refusing to undertake the office of warden for the year).

The ordinances vary in their contents, but display many similarities and common features. The recurring elements are as follows

- A requirement to attend an annual reading of the accounts (with fine for non-compliance).
- A requirement to attend the burial of a fraternity member (with fine for non-compliance).
- A requirement to pay the mass penny for deceased members.
- Imposition of a fine for refusing the office of warden.
- Provision for the lighting of candles at various times.
- Assistance for members who fall into financial hardship.
- Provision for ensuring burial of members who die away from Bridport.

The following table shows how these elements are distributed within the surviving records of the fraternities:

| Fraternity | Annual Meeting | Attend Burial | Mass Penny | Refusal of Wardenship | Lighting of Candles | Relief of distress | Death away from Bridport |
|---|---|---|---|---|---|---|---|
| Light hanging before the Cross | yes | yes | yes | yes | | | |
| St Nicholas | yes | yes | yes | yes | | | |
| Torches (single reference) | | | | yes | | | |
| Two Torches (fragmentary) | yes | | yes | yes | yes | yes | |
| Holy Cross | yes | yes | | | yes | yes | yes |
| St. Mary & St. James | | yes | yes | | yes | yes | yes |

*DC-BTB/CD/56: Ordinances of the Fraternity of St Mary and St James.*

In every case members of the fraternities were required to swear a "corporal oath" to abide by these ordinances – this involved touching a book of the Gospels while swearing, an act of great solemnity.

It is not just within Bridport that the fraternity ordinances show so many recurring elements. In 1870 the antiquarian Joshua Toulmin Smith published "The Original Ordinances of more than one hundred Early English Gilds", which demonstrate that, with local variations, the same broad themes can be found in the rules of the parish fraternities across England.

These themes reflect some of the main reasons why individuals were motivated to join parish fraternities. Among such reasons was the widespread belief that holding masses for deceased members was a powerful means of easing their progress through Purgatory. Another was a belief in the efficacy of honouring a particular saint by activities such as keeping a candle burning before an image in the church. This had a "transactional" element – the saints were expected to reward those who honoured their images by looking after them in this life and the next. The uncertainty of life in late mediaeval England inclined many to participate in such practices.

*3.5 The Annual Meeting for Accounts and the Election of Wardens*
The records of their annual meetings also differ relatively little from fraternity to fraternity. The outgoing wardens account to the members for their year in office. The next year's wardens are then elected. Before looking in more detail at the evidence concerning these meetings, it is worth considering this key role of warden.

All the fraternities without exception seem to have used the title *custos* or "warden" to denote these annually appointed office holders. They were responsible for the finances of the fraternity. It will be seen from the various types of income and expenditure discussed in 3.6 below that this was not a simple task. In order to safeguard fraternity funds, each elected warden had to be backed by two or more "pledges" or "sureties" who acted as their guarantors.

In the records of three of the Bridport fraternities, the term "steward" *(senescallus)* also occurs but the relationship between this office and that of the warden is far from clear. The Fraternity of the Two Torches recorded the election of stewards specifically to oversee fund-raising Ales. In the case of the Fraternities of the Blessed Virgin Mary and the Holy Cross, it seems that stewards were elected who, in their turn, elected the wardens – the stewards of the Fraternity of the Blessed Virgin Mary put their name to the more detailed accounts that have survived for this body (see 3.6 below), and were named as parties in two of the four title deeds relating to this fraternity – but, confusingly, it is the wardens who are named as parties in the other two.

In addition to their financial responsibilities, the wardens were responsible for maintaining discipline in their fraternity, and for levying fines on members who failed to adhere to the ordinances. It is perhaps not surprising that some members sought to avoid such responsibilities. Mediaeval offices might well be perceived as a burden at one particular stage of a person's life, and welcomed at another. Refusal to accept election by the brothers and sisters to the wardenship had its consequences, as is specifically laid out in several of the surviving ordinances. In the records of the

Fraternity of the Torches, it seems that a number of members chose to pay a fine of one pound of wax rather than accept "the burden of the wardenship", (DC-BTB/CD/15/5). The numbers of wardens elected varies from fraternity to fraternity, most electing two or three each year. The Fraternity of the Torches seems to have begun by appointing three annual wardens, but during the period of their accounts this number increases first to four, then to five, and even on one occasion to six. The Fraternity of the Blessed Virgin Mary is something of an outlier in this matter, the surviving records seeming to suggest that a large group of up to ten wardens were chosen annually.

Each fraternity had its chosen day for holding the annual meeting, though for some this seemed to vary over time. With some exceptions the account of each annual meeting is dated. The following table shows the days on which the fraternities usually met and the period covered by their surviving records (no records exist for the annual meetings of the Fraternity of the Mortuary Lights).

| Fraternity | Usual date annual meeting held | Date range of records of annual meetings | Comments |
|---|---|---|---|
| Light hanging before the Cross | Sunday after Christmas | 1425 - 1462 | Mostly continuous, but with some undated meetings and some single year gaps |
| St Nicholas | Day of Holy Innocents | 1423 - 1437 | Mostly continuous |
| Torches | Palm Sunday | 1424 - 1457 | Continuous |
| Two Torches | Tuesday after Easter | 1419 - 1481 | Mostly continuous up to 1460 (either one or two year intervals) and then three isolated entries for 1467, 1477 and 1481 |
| St. Katherine | 1) St. Thomas Day 2) St John the Apostle Day 3) Feast of Circumcision | 1428 - 1479 | Continuous 1428 to 1436, then gap. Continuous 1452 to 1459, then gap. Continuous 1466 to 1471 with single entry for 1479. |
| Blessed Virgin Mary | 1) week after Epiphany 2) Sunday after Purification 3) Sunday before Purification 4) Sunday after Epiphany | 1462 - 1475 | No continuous record of meetings. Some undated sessions, some sessions dated but not chronologically ordered. |
| Holy Cross | Sunday after Epiphany | 1400 - 1475 | The meetings from 1400 to 1421 are summarised in the Wainwright translation (from lost documents). Meetings for 1470 and 1473 – 1475 are recorded in CD50. |

| Fraternity | Meeting date | Date Range | Comments |
|---|---|---|---|
| St. Mary & St. James | 1) Sunday after St Botolph 2) Sunday after St Thomas the Martyr 3) Sunday after Purification | 1407 - 1455 | Continuous 1407 to 1415, then gap to 1436. Continuous to 1440, then isolated entries for 1444 and 1455. |

*Day of the Holy Innocents, 28 December; Palm Sunday, the Sunday before Easter; St Thomas (the Apostle), 21 December; St John the Apostle, 27 December; Feast of the Circumcision, 1 January; Epiphany, 6 January; the Purification of the Blessed Virgin, 2 February; St Botolph, 17 June; St Thomas the Martyr, 29 December.*

From records across the country it seems that these annual meetings were sociable affairs, involving eating and drinking once the business had been conducted. It is likely that this was true of the Bridport fraternities also, although the only surviving evidence for this is a passage within the records of the Fraternity of the Torches, where it is stated: "Also it is ordained that, by the common assent of all the brothers and sisters of the said fraternity, the aforesaid wardens should pay for a luncheon on the day of the accounting, three pence on bread, and three gallons of good beer." (It is relevant to mention at this point that the holding of an annual feast on the patronal saint's day, a custom which appears in innumerable records and accounts of fraternities across England, is also absent from the Bridport records).

Nowhere in the Bridport records is there a clear reference to any kind of "guild hall" or of any building owned by the fraternities which could serve as a meeting place. It seems that the venues might vary from year to year - the ordinances of the Fraternity of St Nicholas state that "each brother or sister should come annually to give a faithful hearing to the reading of the accounts…. at a suitable place agreed by the wardens of the said fraternity."

There are a couple of interesting references within the records of the Fraternity of the Torches, as follows:

"On this day, in the house of John Brode and Nicholas Adam, that is to say Palm Sunday 1457, the aforesaid wardens came and heard the account, that is to say of the aforesaid fraternity." And the following year: "On this day, in the house of John Mayyow, that is to say Palm Sunday 1458, the aforesaid wardens came and heard the account, that is to say of the aforesaid fraternity."

Given that all fraternity members were required to attend the annual meeting, this may imply that there was a separate audit meeting at which the wardens audited the account in a private house, while the main meeting was subsequently held elsewhere.

### 3.6 Financial records

The financial records are fragmentary and an overall assessment of the finances of the Bridport fraternities is accordingly very difficult. In many cases we have only the record of the sums of money accounted for by the outgoing wardens at the annual meeting, and the sums received from them by the new wardens.

In common with fraternities elsewhere in the country (see 2.4) the Bridport fraternities obtained their income from a number of different sources, including bequests, entrance fees, fines, rental income from land and properties, and fundraising efforts such as the holding of "ales". They spent this income on items such as wax for the candles, paying priests to perform masses, purchasing food and drink, and meeting expenses connected with the fraternities' ownership of land and properties.

Only in the case of the Fraternity of the Blessed Virgin Mary do we have anything approaching more detailed financial records, although these are very fragmentary in nature. The accounts of this fraternity for the years 1461/2 and 1475/6 give a sample of the sources of income, which include:

- Membership subscriptions : "Next they answer for groats collected from the brothers and sisters the same year 23s 2d".
- Money raised at a social event: "Next for ale sold the same year 12s".
- Bequests: "Next they answer for the legacy of Nicholas Stevyns' sister 3d".
- Rental income from livestock: "Next he answers for the rent of one cow for a year, in the keeping of the wife of J. Boleyn 20s".

The accounts for these same years also show the wardens asking for allowance to be made for any loss of income or expenses that they have incurred in respect of:

- Arrears:  "Next they ask for sums to be allowed: firstly for arrears in the last accounts, as is shown in a schedule £3 16d".
- Expenditure on maintaining fraternity properties: "Next they ask to be allowed, as is shown in a schedule, for the repair of 2 cottages of Sir John Wyne £13 8s 6d".
- Rents payable on fraternity properties: "Next for the rent due to the King for the tenement of Denis Tayler 3d".
- Expenditure on entertaining: "Next for bread, wine and beer 3d".

These more detailed accounts (which unfortunately have not survived for any of the other Bridport fraternities), provide a tantalisingly brief glimpse into the activities of these bodies throughout the year and the responsibilities of the wardens or stewards for managing their funds.

## 3.7 Title Deeds

Finally we have included in the translation of fraternity documents a number of title deeds, in which particular fraternities are named as one of the parties, whether as grantor / lessor or as grantee / lessee.

There are sixteen separate catalogue items in the Bridport Borough archive included here which record fraternity involvement in the transfer of property. Two of these, dating to the first half of the fourteenth century, relate to the Fraternity of the Mortuary Lights at St Mary's, the only evidence of this fraternity. A series of five items, covering a range of dates from 1356 to 1493, record transactions of the Fraternity of St Katherine at St. Mary's. A further series of four, with dates from 1443 to 1528, relate to the Fraternity of the Blessed Virgin Mary. A final series of five, which concern the Fraternity of the Holy Trinity at St Andrew's Chapel, represent the earliest records of fraternities in Bridport, dating to the thirteenth century.

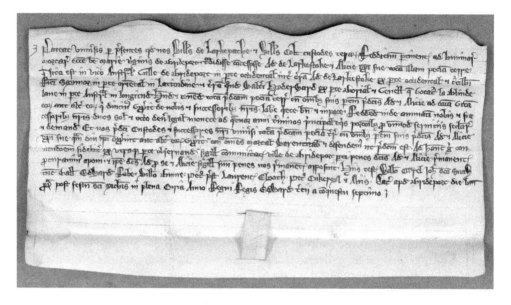

*DC-BTB/CD/12b: Title deed: lease by the wardens of the Fraternity of the Mortuary Lights of land in South Street, 1333.*

The sixteen items containing fraternity title deeds are summarised below.

| Item no | Date | Fraternity | Nature of Transaction |
|---|---|---|---|
| CD12 | 1333 | Mortuary Lights | The fraternity wardens grant a lease for land in South Street to Adam and Alice de Larkestock for the term of their lives. |
| CD13 | 1342 | Mortuary Lights | Nicholas de Chideoc confirms his father's grant to the fraternity wardens of the rent from a West Street tenement |
| CD23 | 1356-1381 | St Katherine | Various transactions relating to two properties in Killings Lane, granted by two separate donors to the fraternity wardens, and subsequently let by those wardens to John and Joan Benesfeld. The rent from these properties is specifically intended to fund the employment of a chaplain. |
| CD24 | 1369 | St Katherine | The chaplain of St Katherine's Chantry grants half the profit of his dovecot to Robert and Alice Beminster. |
| CD25 | 1387 | St Katherine | The Chaplain of St Katherine's Chantry concedes to John and Joan Benesfeld the reversion of an East Street property. |
| CD26 | 1487 | St Katherine | Cofferers of the Borough let a tenement in South Street to the chaplain of St Katherine's Chantry. |

| | | | |
|---|---|---|---|
| CD27 | 1493 | St Katherine | John Burgh grants two burgage plots in East Street to the Bridport bailiffs, with all profits to go to the chaplain of St Katherine's Chantry |
| CD34 | 1475 | Blessed Virgin Mary | Fraternity stewards let a tenement in East Street to William and Joan Cornysh |
| CD35 | 1475 | Blessed Virgin Mary | Fraternity stewards let land in St Michael's Lane to John and Alice Bremell |
| CD36 | 1443 | Blessed Virgin Mary | Fraternity wardens let a tenement in South Street to Henry Harman |
| CD37 | 1528 | Blessed Virgin Mary | Fraternity wardens let a barn in Irish Lane and half an acre of land to Stephen Kirsey |
| CD51 | 1271 | Holy Trinity | Deeds relating to the lease by William Killing to Eudo the merchant, cofferer to the fraternity, of a dwelling house in East Street for a term of eight years. |
| CD52 | undated C.13th | Holy Trinity | Eudo the merchant, cofferer to the fraternity, lets the same property and also some land in South Street to Henry Krideton, the rent to be for the benefit of St Mary's church and the Abbeys of Abbotsbury and Forde. |
| CD53 | undated C.13th | Holy Trinity | Matilda de Staldeford confirms the grant of two houses in South Street to the fraternity, the rent from the houses to support the employment of a chaplain, and to make donations to the Abbeys of Abbotsbury and Forde. |
| CD54 | undated C.13th | Holy Trinity | Thomas de Sule grants a dwelling house by the eastern bridge of the town to the fraternity |
| CD55 | undated C.13th | Holy Trinity | Mabel Maulard grants four pence annual rent to the fraternity. |

## 4 The Bridport Fraternities – the Members

What, if anything, can be learned from the surviving records about the individual members of the Bridport fraternities? In preparing this volume 612 named individuals were identified as fraternity members (the Mortuary Lights and Holy Trinity Fraternities, for which no membership lists have survived, are excluded). This has inevitably involved a considerable amount of uncertainty. Within the records there are a number of similar or even identical names. Having established that the bearers of these names were living in Bridport at roughly the same period, a "best guess" has to be made as to whether or not they refer to the same individual. With that caveat, the spreadsheet has made possible the collection of information about each individual fraternity member, as follows: their gender; to which fraternity or fraternities they belonged; and whether they served as wardens or as pledges for a warden. To this information gathered from the fraternity records, it has sometimes been possible to add some further details about individuals from other sources, such as lists of Bridport burgesses, court records, the account book of Munden's Chantry, and other documents from the Bridport Borough Collection as recorded in the Historical Manuscripts Commission report.

*4.1 Gender*

Membership lists show that both men and women could be members of the fraternities. When speaking of the membership the records routinely refer to "fratres et sorores" (brothers and sisters). Out of the 612 named individuals identified, a total of 248 (41%) are female. Women, however, are almost always listed by reference to their husbands – a typical entry would be "Johannes Borage et Agneta uxor eius" (John Borage and Agnes his wife). Where women are listed separately it is usually clear that they are widows, rather than unmarried people.

With one exception, the Bridport fraternities differ relatively little in the balance of men and women in the surviving membership lists. The records of all but one fraternity have a percentage of female names between 38% (St Mary & St James) and 47% (The Torches), most having percentages in the low forties. For the Fraternity of the Blessed Virgin Mary only 18% of recorded members are female, but the names for this fraternity are taken from a mass penny list rather than a membership list, and it may be that spouses of contributing members have been omitted.

Unsurprisingly, given the male-dominated nature of mediaeval society, out of 119 individuals named as accepting the office of warden, a position which clearly implied the respect and confidence of the fraternity membership, no fewer than 114 were male. The five exceptions, therefore, come as a surprise and merit a closer look.

In June 1434, Henry Gamelyn was elected as warden for the Fraternity of St Katherine, and re-elected for the following two years. There then follows a long gap in the sequence of annual entries, which resume eighteen years later in June 1452, when we read: "*Venerunt Iohannes Burges et Iohanna nuper uxor Henrici Gamelyn custodes fraternitatis Sancte Katerine predicte et reddiderunt compotum suum..*" , (John Burges and Joan, widow of Henry Gamelyn, wardens of the said Fraternity of St. Katherine, came and rendered their account). Because of the break in the record, we have no way of knowing if this was Joan Gamelyn's first and indeed only year of office (she was not re-elected in 1453).

At the Christmas gatherings of the Fraternity of the Light Hanging before the Cross, in both 1454 and 1455, John Atkyn was elected as warden for the coming year. But he must have died during his second year of office, since he was replaced at the following year's reading of accounts by his widow, Margaret. That it was not simply a matter of Margaret Atkyn completing and reporting on her late husband's year of duty is clearly shown by the fact that she was duly elected as warden in her own right for each of the following five years until 1461.

On three occasions in the mid 1450s the Fraternity of the Torches selected John and Isabell Croll, apparently as a joint appointment, to the wardenship. This is the only instance in the records of a married couple taking this role jointly.

The other two recorded female wardens, Isabel Mayyow and Joan Brownys, are both in the records as being chosen alongside no fewer than eight other wardens at meetings of the Fraternity of the Blessed Virgin Mary – undated but probably in the

1470s. The exceptional nature of this fraternity's large warden group has already been referred to.

It would be good to know more about these five women of Bridport and their status in the town. But it is certainly worthy of note that in this male-dominated world they could command sufficient respect to be elected to this post and entrusted with its attendant responsibilities. Elsewhere it is possible to find parallels to these officers in the women who were elected as churchwardens in late mediaeval and Tudor Somerset: these officers were also usually widows who served in a rotation based around property holding.[25]

### 4.2 Social Status and Occupation

It was noted above in 2.3 that in many towns across England membership of particular fraternities suggested a higher social ranking. Was this true of Bridport? One clue can be provided by comparing lists of the bailiffs of the town with the fraternity membership lists.[26] A total of 20 individual fraternity members can be identified as having served in the office of bailiff, the pinnacle of civic life. Of these, 13 were members of the Fraternity of St Katherine, 12 of the Fraternity of the Blessed Virgin Mary, and 10 of the Fraternity of the Holy Cross (these numbers include multiple membership). Other fraternities have far lower instances of bailiff membership, suggesting that the three fraternities mentioned above were particularly appealing to the upper levels of the town hierarchy. At the lower end of the spectrum the Fraternities of St Nicholas (3 bailiff members), St. Mary & St James (2) and The Torches (1) may have been seen as offering fewer opportunities for social advancement.

The occupations of fraternity members are only rarely mentioned in the fraternity documents themselves. There are occasional instances where an occupational term is added to an individual's name – in the Holy Cross records, for example, one John Homan is frequently described as "butcher" – but these are few and far between. Occupations can, however, sometimes be discovered by reference to other contemporary sources, in particular the court lists, the household accounts of the Munden Chantry and other documents in the Borough Archive.

Members for whom occupations can be tentatively identified in this way number 75. Higher status occupations include: clergy (14 occurrences); merchants (7); and single instances of a tailor, a yeoman and a gentleman. Craftsmen include: suppliers of building materials, including to the Munden chantry priests (13); butchers (6); ropers (5); and one or two instances each of dyers, glovers and carpenters. Other occupations include agricultural workers or husbandmen (10); chapmen: (4); and single examples of fishermen and servants.

Can any correlation be made between particular occupations and fraternity membership? It appears that the most popular fraternities both for those identified as suppliers of building material to the Munden priests and for those described as "merchants" were the Fraternities of the Two Torches, St Katherine, the Blessed Virgin Mary and the Holy Cross. Only isolated individuals from these categories can be found

---

25   French, 'Women Churchwardens in late Medieval England'.
26   The names of all bailiffs and cofferers from Dorset History Centre, DC-BTB/M/11

among the membership lists of the Fraternities of the Light Hanging Before the Cross, the Torches, St Nicholas or St. Mary & St James. The largest numbers of husbandmen members are found in the Fraternities of the Holy Cross, the Light Hanging Before the Cross, and St Mary & St James. The surviving records do not permit any firm conclusions, but suggest that variations did exist in the range of occupations held by members of the different fraternities.

     The clergy form an interesting sub-set of the membership. A total of 14 members are named as clergy. Their names are generally found at the head of the membership lists. Nine of these can be identified as clergy only by their honorific title "Dominus", translated as "Sir" (this is the "Sir" used by Shakespeare for characters such as Sir Topaz in Twelfth Night - not to be confused with the "Sir" of knighthood). The roles that these nine individuals performed in the church life of Bridport are not known. The majority of these nine were members of the Fraternity of the Torches and the Fraternity of the Blessed Virgin Mary. Of the other five, four are named as chaplains of the chantry of St Katherine in St Mary's church. They were members of the St Katherine's Fraternity and were directly employed as priests by the fraternity members. (This arrangement is confirmed by the title deed DC/BTB/CD/24, translated in this volume, which records the grant of two properties to the St Katherine's wardens, the profits from the properties being intended to fund the employment of a chaplain).This is evidence of a Bridport fraternity being wealthy enough to employ a full-time priest, a common enough arrangement elsewhere in the country. The only other evidence for this in Bridport is found in the much earlier thirteenth century title deed of the Fraternity of the Holy Trinity, DC-BTB/CD/53, where some houses were granted to the fraternity to support a chaplain. The fifth clergyman whose role is known was a rector of Bridport, Sir John Helier, a member of the Torches Fraternity (this individual will be mentioned again below in the section on individual lives, 4.6).

*4.3 Multiple Membership*
It can be seen from the records that many individuals chose to belong to more than one fraternity. The relatively low cost of joining and the social benefits it conveyed obviously made multiple membership both possible and desirable. Did this differ between fraternities? Did some have a higher percentage of "one fraternity only" members? The following table seeks to address this question :

| | Total members | Member 1 Frat | Member 2 Frats | Member 3 Frats | Member 4 Frats | Member 5 Frats | Member 6 Frats |
|---|---|---|---|---|---|---|---|
| Light hanging before the Cross | 98 | 29 (30%) | 19 (19%) | 25 (26%) | 17 (17%) | 6 (6%) | 2 (2%) |
| St Nicholas | 60 | 13 (22%) | 11 (18%) | 19 (32%) | 13 (22%) | 2 (3%) | 2 (3%) |

| | | | | | | | |
|---|---|---|---|---|---|---|---|
| Torches | 120 | 72 (60%) | 24 (20%) | 7 (6%) | 11 (9%) | 4 (3%) | 2 (2%) |
| Two Torches | 124 | 49 (40%) | 32 (26%) | 21 (17%) | 17 (14%) | 5 (4%) | 0 |
| St. Katherine | 118 | 50 (42%) | 26 (22%) | 24 (20%) | 11 (9%) | 5 (4%) | 2 (2%) |
| Blessed Virgin Mary | 113 | 60 (53%) | 23 (20%) | 17 (15%) | 10 (9%) | 3 (3%) | 0 |
| Holy Cross | 204 | 108 (53%) | 42 (21%) | 28 (14%) | 18 (9%) | 6 (3%) | 2 (1%) |
| St. Mary & St. James | 91 | 43 (47%) | 19 (21%) | 12 (13%) | 11 (12%) | 4 (4%) | 2 (2%) |

It can be seen that five of the eight fraternities for whom membership lists exist had between 40% and 53% of their members who did not belong to any other fraternities. The Fraternity of the Torches had the highest percentage of "single fraternity" members (60%). The lowest percentages are found in the Fraternities of the Light Hanging before the Cross (30%) and the Fraternity of St Nicholas (22%), perhaps suggesting that these were popular choices for those wishing to network over more than one fraternity.

Some caution is necessary in interpreting these figures, as the membership lists of the different fraternities were drawn up at different times, so it is impossible in some cases to be certain whether a particular individual was simultaneously a member of several fraternities or whether he or she had left one fraternity to join another. Nonetheless it is clear that it was common for people to be members of several fraternities during their lives. Brown summarises this situation; "The fraternities of Bridport, in the parish of St. Mary, were made up of close-knit, overlapping groups of parishioners".[27]

*4.4 Office Holders*

As previously described, within each fraternity a number of members emerged from "the ranks" to assume the office of warden, sometimes for a single year, sometimes for longer periods. Others agreed to be the "pledges", acting as guarantors of the wardens for the year. Comparing the record of those who took on these responsibilities with the wider membership lists suggests possible differences between the fraternities as to whether leadership roles were widely shared or restricted to a few members.

As has already been shown the holding of positions of responsibility within the fraternities was almost exclusively a matter for men (see 4.1, where the five exceptions, women who served as warden, are discussed). The following table shows the numbers and percentage of men in each fraternity who i) served as wardens , ii) served as either warden or as pledge or both, and iii) never took office (member only).

27  Brown, *Popular Piety*, p.137

| | Total membership (male only) | Served as Warden | | Served as either Warden or Pledge or both | | Member only | |
|---|---|---|---|---|---|---|---|
| Light hanging before the Cross | 59 | 30 | (51%) | 42 | (71%) | 17 | (29%) |
| St Nicholas | 35 | 22 | (63%) | 26 | (74%) | 9 | (26%) |
| Torches | 63 | 27 | (43%) | 36 | (57%) | 27 | (43%) |
| Two Torches | 73 | 34 | (47%) | 52 | (71%) | 21 | (29%) |
| St. Katherine | 66 | 31 | (47%) | 47 | (71%) | 19 | (29%) |
| Blessed Virgin Mary | 93 | 29 | (31%) | 43 | (46%) | 50 | (54%) |
| Holy Cross | 120 | 41 | (34%) | 62 | (52%) | 58 | (48%) |
| St. Mary & St. James | 56 | 24 | (43%) | 34 | (61%) | 22 | (39%) |

The Fraternity of St Nicholas, shown in the previous section to have had the highest percentage of members who joined other fraternities, emerges here as the fraternity with the highest percentage of members who served as warden or as pledge for a warden, perhaps suggesting a high degree of participation in the running of the fraternity. The Fraternity of the Blessed Virgin Mary, at the other end of the spectrum, shows the lowest percentage of members taking these roles, perhaps indicating a tendency to limit positions of responsibility to a smaller group.

### 4.5 Individual lives

For the great majority of the 612 named residents of mediaeval Bridport who were involved in fraternities, the details of their lives, other than the bare facts of their fraternity membership, are unknown and unknowable. For a few, however, whose names can fortuitously be found in other contemporary sources, it is possible to add a few more details which demonstrate the wide range of society from which the members were drawn.

Many fraternity members are recorded in other documents of the fifteenth century as having been involved in court cases, often as defendants in debt proceedings.[28] For example, John Boleyn, a merchant who belonged to four fraternities, appeared

---

28   The following examples are drawn from the indexes to the Court of Common Pleas on the Anglo-American Legal Tradition website, http://aalt.law.uh.edu/IndexPri.html (accessed 11/7/2022).

in court for debt nine times between 1440 and 1458. One of the relatively few named members of the clergy to appear as a fraternity member was Sir John Helier, rector of St Mary's and a member of the Torches Fraternity. He appeared no fewer than fifteen times as a defendant for debt between 1430 and 1463. William House was a husbandman and a member of five fraternities, who served as warden for several of them. He found himself in court for debt on a number of occasions between 1444 and 1465.

Other fraternity members appearing in the court include John Beer, a husbandman who was a member of the Torches and Holy Cross Fraternities, who was charged with assault in 1430. Emota Butt, a member of three fraternities, was presented before the court in 1460 for causing nuisance outside her premises in several streets. William Edmunde (Fraternity of the Blessed Virgin Mary) was charged in 1470 with killing a horse.

Sir John Helier, rector of Bridport and Torches Fraternity member, already mentioned for his involvement in debt cases, was the subject of an inquisition by the church authorities in 1441, for his refusal to maintain a chaplain at St Andrews, along with other complaints from the bailiffs and community.[29]

The detailed account book for Munden's chantry (1453-1460) provides the opportunity to see the members of different fraternities interacting with another Bridport institution over a number of years. It mentions the names of several fraternity members. Some are named as tradesmen or suppliers of material to the chantry priests. Examples include John Bittisgate (Two Torches and Holy Cross Fraternities) who sold them timber and other building material; John Butt (member of four fraternities) whom they paid for 4000 shingles and for transport; and John Hulle (member of three fraternities) whom the Munden priests paid for the repair of various houses.

Others are named as visitors to the priests' home. Sir John Spyney, a member of the St Katherine's Fraternity and one of the priests employed by that fraternity as a chaplain visited the priests for dinner. On another occasion wine was bought for visitors who included John Atkyn (member of three fraternities) and William Olyver, a merchant who was a member of no fewer than five fraternities. William Olyver was clearly a significant figure in the town, serving as bailiff on three occasions and having been responsible for the fund-raising effort in 1454 (recorded in DC-BTB/CD/6) when he collected money from a number of fraternities and went to London to purchase antiphonals (music books) for the church. One woman, Mabel Wodewale (Holy Cross Fraternity) is mentioned as having frequent dealings with the Munden priests as a landowner. The exact relationship is not clear, but the priests record several payments to her in respect of various tenements. On one occasion a "Mabel" is recorded as coming to dine at the house with her son, John - but this may have been a different person (perhaps a relative of one of the priests).

The fact that a number of fraternity members served as town bailiffs allows us, from time to time, a glimpse of their activities in this leading municipal role. Three fraternity members, John Bittisgate (Two Torches and Holy Cross Fraternities), Stephen Davey (member and warden of three fraternities) and John Harrys (Blessed

29   H.M.C. sixth report, 495

Virgin Mary and Holy Cross Fraternities) are named as being bailiffs involved in the project to restore Bridport harbour in 1447. Another bailiff, William Milleward (member of four fraternities) is recorded as having made the journey to London to purchase manacles, and as having been recompensed for the costs incurred. Robert Scarlet (St Katherine's Fraternity) was clearly a prominent citizen – he is mentioned in the records as having received money from William Olyver, as having acted as constable and, as bailiff, as having overseen the cleaning of the town ditch which formed the northern boundary of the town, approximately following the line of Rax Lane today.

The great majority of the fraternity members recorded in the surviving documents are known only as names. The small and random snippets of information that can be gleaned about a few of them from other sources serve only to shed a very small amount of light on the lives of these 612 people who lived their lives in Bridport during the late mediaeval period.

### 5. Description of the Documents

The documents translated in this book, all contained within the Bridport Borough collection at the Dorset History Centre, have survived in a variety of forms. Some are in the form of small books, with paper sheets bound within covers of various types. Others, such as the title deeds, are single documents often in parchment. They vary greatly in condition, some in an excellent state of preservation, others having suffered considerable damage.

### 5.1  *Form and condition*

The following table summarises the form and condition of the documents translated in this volume.

| *Document* | *Fraternity* | *Date (range)* | *Form of Document* | *Condition* |
|---|---|---|---|---|
| CD6 | Various | 1454 | Two small paper documents | fair, some staining and damage to edges |
| CD11 | Light hanging before the Cross | 1425-1461 | Small book, 18 pages. The front and back covers are of parchment recycled from other manuscripts | good |
| CD12-13 | Mortuary Lights | 1333-1342 | Three separate title deeds | good |
| CD14 | St Nicholas | 1423-1437 | Small book, 10 pages | good |
| CD15 | Torches | 1425-1461 | Small book, 20 pages. The front and back covers are of parchment recycled from a manuscript of church music | fair |

| CD16 | Two Torches | 1419-1480 | Small book, 20 pages | first page fragment only, another page incomplete, otherwise good |
|---|---|---|---|---|
| CD22 | St. Katherine | 1428 - 1479 | Small book, 19 pages | Some pages very fragile, mostly fair |
| CD23 - 27 | St. Katherine | 1356-1493 | Ten separate title deeds | Mostly good or fair, one badly torn |
| CD31 - 33 | Blessed Virgin Mary | 1462 - 1475 | Nine unbound sheets | First sheet badly damaged, remainder good |
| CD34 - 37 | Blessed Virgin Mary | 1443 - 1528 | Four title deeds | good |
| CD50 | Holy Cross | 1470 - 1474 | Two unbound sheets | good |
| CD51 - 55 | Holy Trinity | late 13c | Seven title deeds | Two are in very poor condition, with holes. Remainder good |
| CD56 | St. Mary & St. James | 1406-1454 | Small book, 7 pages | good |

## 5.2 Language

The documents presented in this volume are, with only a few exceptions, in Latin. The  exceptions, all in the English of the day, are: the account of William Olyver's fundraising from the fraternities for the purchase of music books for the church (DC-BTB/CD/6);  the fragment of a sermon found towards the end of the St Nicholas Fraternity records  (DC-BTB/CD/14 p.9); a fragment, of only three lines, of a note concerning the delivery of a sum of money to one Walter Threder, within the St Katherine's records  (DC-BTB/CD/22 p.18) ; and an account of monies received by the Fraternity of the Blessed Virgin Mary  (DC-BTB/CD/33).

While Latin was a normal language of record-keeping during the late mediaeval period, the use of English in administrative records was gradually increasing. It is notable that a large number of the returns made by parish fraternities to the government of Richard II in 1389 (see 3.5 above), collected and published by the Victorian scholar Joshua Toulmin Smith, were in English. Typically the returns would begin with a preamble in Latin, but English would often be used for the details of their "ordinances". It can safely be assumed that the Bridport fraternities conducted their business meetings in English and that the ordinances or rules of each fraternity would have been made known in that language to members, whose knowledge of Latin may have been minimal. The fact that the surviving records are almost exclusively in Latin, therefore, may be seen as reflecting a certain conservatism among the fraternities in this part of England.

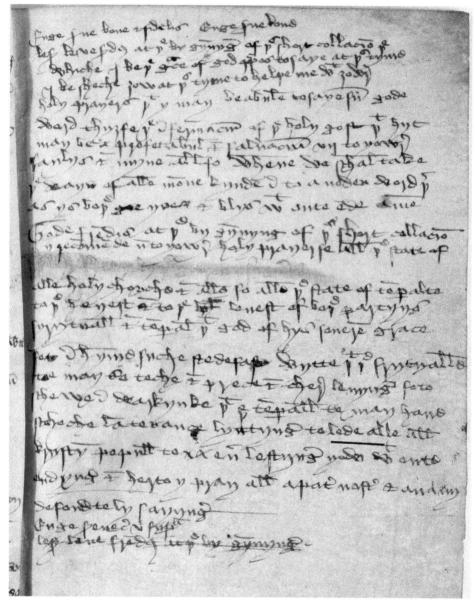

*DC-BTB/CD/15: part of a sermon in English at the end of a volume of annual accounts relating to the Fraternity of St Nicholas*

The Latin used by the scribes of Bridport in the fourteenth and fifteenth centuries was not the Latin of classical Rome, but was a working language with many imported words needed to express concepts that were important at the time, such as *warrantizare* (to warrant or guarantee), *tofta* (a toft or plot of land on which a house and out-buildings stood), or *cotagium* (a cottage).

Grammatical mistakes occur from time to time. For example, in the records of the Fraternity of St Nicholas for 1429-1430 (DC-BTB/CD/14 p.6) the scribe has written *et electi fuerunt novos custodes* (and new wardens were elected), whereas correct Latin grammar would require *electi fuerunt novi custodes.* The convention of abbreviating Latin words by omitting their endings undoubtedly allowed the scribes to avoid having to make too many decisions about Latin grammar.

It seems that the scribes were sometimes at a loss to express themselves clearly in Latin and resorted to the inclusion of an English word. In the accounts of the Fraternity of the Blessed Virgin Mary we find:

| | | |
|---|---|---|
| *Item pro duobus cruets* | *v d* | (for two cruets, 5d) |
| *Item pro C latchys* | *viij d* | (for 100 latches, 8d) |
| *Item pro iiii C naylys* | *vj d* | (for 400 nails, 6d) |
| *Item pro mille pynys* | *iij d* | (for 1000 pins 3d). |

Kathleen Wood-Legh, in the Introduction to her published transcription of the account book of the Munden Chantry priests, makes the convincing suggestion, as an explanation of this phenomenon, that "the Latin word he (the priest writing the accounts) wanted had, for the moment, escaped his memory, a possibility which deserves more consideration than it usually receives when the knowledge of Latin of people who wrote it without the aid of dictionaries is estimated".[30]

*5.3 Handwriting*

The handwriting of the documents and the conventional abbreviations used can present as much if not more of a challenge as the Latin. Unsurprisingly, changes can be seen in the handwriting over the centuries covered in this volume – for example the earliest documents, those of the Fraternity of the Holy Trinity, which date from the late 13th century, show the characteristically elaborate "beaver-tailed s" of that period, a feature which is not seen in the later fourteenth and fifteenth century documents.

As previously mentioned, scribes routinely abbreviated the endings of words with a variety of squiggles and flourishes. A passage such as *Memorandum quod in dominica die ante festum Purificationis Beate Marie Virginis anno regni regis Edwardi iiiiti vicesimo....* (Let it be noted that on the Sunday before the Purification of the Blessed Virgin Mary in the twentieth year of the reign of King Edward IV....) is in fact written *Md qd in dmca die ant fm Purificacois be Marie Vgis Ao r r E iiijti vicesimo.....*, requiring the reader to supply the missing endings from the context and knowledge of the conventional abbreviations.

The quality of the handwriting varies considerably. In general it can be said that the title deeds, being documents of legal importance, are clearly and carefully written. Some of the most attractive handwriting in the documents covered in this book is found in the lists of fraternity members, some of which (such as those of the Fraternities of St Nicholas and St Mary & St James) begin with beautifully decorated capital letters. Over the course of time, however, the appearance of these lists is often marred by crossings out, presumably as members die or otherwise leave the fraternity. The ordinances of the fraternities are also often written in a fine hand, reflecting

30  Wood-Legh, *A Small Household,* p.xiii

their importance to the members.

Less care is generally taken in the reports of the annual meetings which record the accounting of the outgoing wardens and the election of new ones. The handwriting of these varies from entry to entry, with many changes of scribe. Some entries are neatly legible, others give the appearance of having been written in haste, with frequent crossings out.

### 5.4 Unrelated material within the documents

Mention needs to be made of a small number of additional pieces of text which are to be found within the fraternity documents but which do not relate directly to the fraternities.

In two instances where fraternity records have been bound together in book form, covers have been created by recycling other manuscripts. Both are of interest.

The records of the Fraternity of the Light Hanging before the Cross (DC-BTB/CD/11) are written on paper but with three pieces of parchment (two at the front, one at the back) used as the cover. The first of the two front covers consist of a parchment, both sides of which have been used at different times. On one side (forming the outside cover of the book) is a fragment of a will, mostly illegible but including legacies to the church of St Mary, Bridport and, intriguingly, to the Fraternity of St. Swithin (the only known reference to this body). The other side of the outer parchment is a fragment (apparently unconnected to the fraternity) of an indenture of apprenticeship from Symondsbury, dating from the reign of Henry IV. Only a section of the document was used for the cover, meaning that the full names of the parties, the exact date and the nature of the apprenticeship are unknown. A certain William is bound as an apprentice to a certain Andrew and Joan for one year from Michaelmas. Surviving terms include an obligation to alert his masters to any damage to their property and a ban on his contracting a marriage during his apprenticeship.

The inner of the two front covers and the back cover consist of three fragmentary pages from a copy of the Customary of Sarum, the manual which prescribes in great detail the way services are to be conducted throughout the year in the diocese of Salisbury. They are written in an attractive hand, with red ink used to highlight certain letters and to underline certain passages. Several revisions were made to the Customary and those which had been superceded were no doubt used as scrap parchment to bind other volumes. Equally, it is possible that it was brought to the town by a priest who had previously been based at Salisbury or it may simply be that the fraternity had acquired an amount of old parchment for recycling.

The book containing the records of the Fraternity of the Torches (DC-BTB/CD/15) is also bound with recycled manuscripts. These are four fragmentary pages of a service book of the 13th century, consisting of extracts from the psalms with musical notation, clearly used for chanting antiphons and responses during church services. It is tempting to suggest that this might be the old "antiphoner" which became surplus to requirements when it was replaced by the new one purchased by William Olyver in 1454, following the fund-raising effort recorded in DC/BTB/CD/6 (the first document translated in the main section of this book).

The final two pages of the book containing the records of the Fraternity of St

Nicholas (DC-BTB/CD/14) also contain material which does not appear to be directly related to the  fraternity's affairs. The two items in question have been included in the translation of documents in this book. The first is the beginning of a sermon, in English, giving us an interesting glimpse of how a Bridport priest of that period might have addressed his flock. The second is the will of one Robert Pewterer, dating from 1451. He leaves money to the rector of St Mary's and to the parish clerk, as well as to the fabric fund of Salisbury Cathedral. He does not, however, leave any money to the fraternity, so the reason for the inclusion of the will among these records is unclear. An Alice Pewterer, possibly his widow, is recorded in the 1467 mass penny list of the Fraternity of the Blessed Virgin Mary.

At the end of the records of the Fraternity of the Two Torches there are some puzzling doodles, which seem to include a repetition of the phrase "Fuit homo missus a Deo" ("There was a man sent by God", lines taken from verse 6 of John's Gospel). Below are a number of doodled names.  "Johannes" seems to appear in various forms. There is also what seems to be a surname "Baktom".

Finally, at the end of the records of the Fraternity of St Mary & St James there is a single doodled name, "Watkin". The reason for this is unknown and unknowable.

## 6. Editorial Conventions

The texts presented in this volume are transcriptions and translations of all the surviving documents produced by the Bridport fraternities in the Bridport Borough Collection (DC-BTB) deposited in the archive at the Dorset History Centre.

Those documents written in English (DC-BTB/CD6/1, CD33) and part of another (DC-BTB/CD/16, page 9) have been transcribed as they are written. Roman numerals have been retained, including where they have been used for sums of money. Abbreviated words have been expanded in square brackets. Capitals and punctuation have been modernised.

All other documents, written in Latin, have been translated into modern English. Surnames and place names have been left in their original forms, forenames have been changed from Latin into their modern English equivalent. Where saints' days and regnal years have been used in manuscript dates their form has been standardised and the modern date supplied in square brackets.

Square brackets have been used to provide additional information, alternative readings, obvious scribal errors and commentary within the text. Round brackets represent manuscript brackets within the text or enclose Latin words and phrases that may be of interest.

Thomas Wainwright's text of the lost book of the Light of the Holy Cross (DC-BTB/PQ/28) has been reproduced as it appears in his manuscript notebook.

For both English and Latin documents superscript has been used to represent inserted manuscript text and a single strike through line to represent words that have been erased but are still legible.

All numerals in Latin documents have been standardised from Roman to Arabic numbers with £ s. d. as standard abbreviations for pounds, shillings and pence.

The abbreviations bsh and qtr(s) have been used for bushel (a capacity measure of grain equivalent to two pints) and quarter (eight bushels).

The hands are typical late mediaeval court hands and mixed hands; often with a different hand used to distinguish the heading from the body of the text. Images have been inserted into the text showing examples of the hands in use in the earlier fifteenth century in the opening folios of DC-BTB/CD/11 (dated 1425), DC-BTB/CD/14 (dated 1423) and DC-BTB/CD/22 (dated 1428) and the English language document DC-BTB/CD/33 (undated, late fifteenth century). The editor has noted where the hand changes to that of a different scribe where it may be of interest, but regular changes in the compilation of accounts have not been noted.

# BIBLIOGRAPHY

Barker, K., *The Bridport Charter of 1253, Making and Meaning* (Bridport History Society and Bridport Charter Fair, 2003).

Brown, A., *Popular Piety in Late Mediaeval England – The Diocese of Salisbury 1250-1550* (Clarendon Press, Oxford, 1995).

Chandler, J. (ed.), *John Leland's Itinerary: Travels in Tudor England* (Alan Sutton, Stroud, 1993).

Duffy, E.: *The Stripping of the Altars – Traditional Religion in England 1400 – 1580* (Yale University Press 1992).

Duffy, E.: *The Voices of Morebath – Reformation and Rebellion in an English Village* (Yale University Press 2001).

Farnhill, K., *Guilds and the Parish Community in Late Medieval East Anglia c.1470 – 1550* (York Medieval Press 2001).

Forrest, M., 'Dorset's trade networks in the 15th century', *Southern History*, (2018), v.40, 24-56.

French, K., 'Women Churchwardens in late Medieval England', in *The Parish in Late Medieval England; Proceedings of the 2002 Harlaxton Symposium*, ed. C. Burgess and E. Duffey (Donnington, Tyas, 2006), Harlaxton series volume 14, 302-21.

Fry, E. A., 'Dorset Chantries' *Proceedings of the Dorset Natural History and Archaeological Society*, (1906), v.27, 214-33; (1907), v.28, 12-29; (1908), v.29, 30-79; (1909), v. 30, 13-57; (1910), v.31, 85-119.

Hindson, R.: *Bridport: Burgh And Borough 878 A.D.-1974 A.D.: A Short History* (Richard Hindson, 1999).

Royal Commission on Historical Manuscripts: *Sixth Report, with Appendix, Part 1* (HMSO, London, 1877).

Royal Commission on Historical Monuments: England, An Inventory of the Historical Monuments in Dorset, Vol.1, West (HMSO, London, 1952).

Penn, K. J., *Historic Towns in Dorset* (Dorchester, 1980) Dorset Natural History and Archaeological Society, Monograph series 1.

Rosser, G.: *The Art of Solidarity in the Middle Ages – Guilds in England 1250 – 1550* (Oxford University Press, 2015).

Toulmin Smith, J.: *English Gilds – the Original Ordinances of More than One Hundred Early English Gilds* (Early English Text Society, 1870).

Victoria History of the Counties of England: *A History of the County of Dorset, Volume 2* (University of London, 1975).

Wainwright, T.: *The Bridport Borough Records and Ancient Manuscripts* (Bridport News, 1900).

Westlake, H. F: *The Parish Gilds of Mediaeval England* (Society for Promoting Christian Knowledge, 1919).

Whitlock, D., (ed.), *English Historical Documents, c.500-1042*, (2nd ed., London: Routledge, 1979).

Wood-Legh, K.L: *A Small Household of the Fifteenth Century* (Manchester University Press, 1956).

# RECORDS OF BRIDPORT FRATERNITIES
## DC-BTB/CD

**CD6.** *Two small documents, dated 1454-1458, relating to a fund-raising campaign to buy two antiphonals or antiphoners [music books] for the church of St Mary, Bridport.*

CD6/1 [English]

This beth the p[ar]cell of money that W. Olyvere hath reseyved of dyv[er]se brotheredynes & other to bye ii antyphonell for our lady chirche of Brydeport anno xxxiii° regni Henry VI<sup>ti</sup> [in the 33<sup>rd</sup> year of the reign of Henry VI, 1454-1455]
First of seynt kat[er]ine ys brothers, xxvijs.
It[em] of the branche, viijs.
It[em] of the crosse leygth at seynt andrywis, xxvjs. viiid.
It[em] of our lady broters, vij marks iijs. iiijd.
It[em] of seynt Thomas is brothers

CD6/2 [Latin]

~~It is to be remembered that on the first Monday in Quadragesima~~ [hole in paper] ~~in the full court William Oliver came~~
It is to be remembered that on the first Monday in Quadragesima [Lent] in 36 Henry VI [1458] William Oliver came in the full court and delivered his account of the money received from various fraternities, that is to say:
For the purchase of an antiphoner, that is to say a *legger* [i.e. ledger]:
Firstly the aforesaid William received from the Fraternity of the Blessed Mary, 7 marks [£4 13s. 4d.].
From the same Fraternity the aforesaid William received £3.
From the same Fraternity the aforesaid William received 16s. 8d.
The aforesaid William received from the Fraternity of the Holy Cross of St Andrew, 26s. 8d.
The aforesaid William received from the Fraternity of St Katherine, 27s.
The aforesaid William received from the light called "Branch", 8s.
In total, £11 11s. 8d.
From this the aforesaid William paid London for 1 ledger, £9 6s. 8d.
So there remains from his audit, 45s. which he delivered to the safe custody of John Wacle of Broad Street, barber, London, in the presence of Thomas Bayly bailliff of the town of Brydeport.

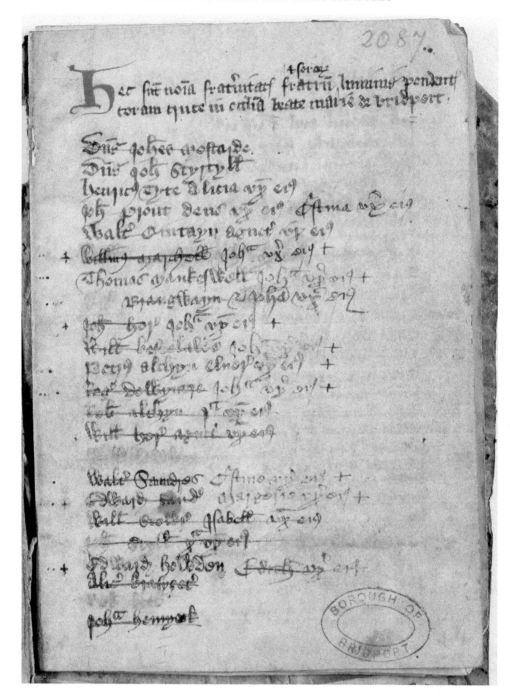

*The first page of DC-BTB/CD/11, naming members of the Fraternity of the Light Hanging before the Cross*

**CD11.** *A small book relating to the Fraternity of the Light Hanging before the Cross, covering period 1425 to 1461. The front and back covers are of parchment recycled from other manuscripts, not directly relating to the Fraternity. These includes pages from a church service book - see Introduction, section 6.2.*

[inside front cover] Symondsbury, on the Thursday after the feast of St Andrew the Apostle, in the year of the reign of King Henry the Fourth after the conquest [blank].

[pages 1-4 blank]

[page 5]
These are the names of the Fraternity of the brothers <sup>and sisters</sup> of the Light Hanging before the Cross in the church of the Blessed Mary of Bridport
Sir John Mostarde
Sir John Styrtyll
Henry Tyte and his wife Alice
John Prout and his wife *Dens* [perhaps *Dionysia*] his wife Cristina
 Walter Quitayn and his wife Agnes
+ William Marchell and his wife Joan +
Thomas Mankeswell and his wife Joan +
[Blank] Brangwayn and his wife Joan
+ John Hore and his wife Joan +
William Bestelawe and his wife Joan +
Peter Alchyn and his wife Elinor +
Roger Dowyntre and his wife Joan +
Robert Alchyn and his wife Joan
William Hore and his wife Agnes
[Blank line – name erased]
Walter Saundres and his wife Christine +
Edward Sander and his wife Margery +
Walter Stowre and his wife Isabel
John Styll and his wife Christine
Edward Howden and his wife Edith
Alice Brasyheter
[Blank line – name erased, perhaps *Robert Bret*]
Joan Hemyok
[page 6]
John Bowdych
Etheldred
+ John Palmer junior and his wife Joan
+ John Chydyocke and his wife Florence
William Parnam and his wife Lettice
John Chylteryn (fined 5d.)
Thomas Schawe (fined 5d.)

Robert Leche
+ Stephen Webbe and his wife Eleanor
Robert Goldhoppe (fined 5d.)
Walter Calwell
Alice Buttes
+ Robert Ayleward and his wife Joan
+ John Atkyn and his wife Margaret
+ ~~John Mankswill and his wife Emota~~
~~William Potell~~ and his wife Alice
~~John Parok and his wife Joan~~
~~William Myllewarde and his wife Joan~~
+John Borage and his wife Agnes
+ John Whyte and his wife Christine
+ John Brode and his wife Alice
+ William Howse and his wife Alice
~~John Keche, hellier~~
+ John Nything and his wife Edith
~~John Chydeock~~ John Dunne, butcher, and Emmota his wife and he paid a fine of 6d.
+ John Beese and his wife Margaret
Nicholas Yung and his wife Joan
Thomas Bayly and his wife Margery 1 pound of wax

[page 7, *Ordinances or rules of the Fraternity*]
It has been has been ordained and agreed between the aforesaid brothers and sisters by common assent as follows: that each brother or sister should come annually to give a faithful hearing to the reading of the accounts, that is to say on the Sunday next after Christmas at a suitable place agreed by the wardens. And if any brother or sister of the Fraternity should abstain from or keep away from the meeting, he or she should pay half a pound of wax. It is also ordained that all brothers and sisters should come to the Mass on the day of the burial of any deceased brother or sister and if possible to the Office for the Dead, and that they should make an offering with them at the aforesaid mass, the above penalty to be applied in the absence of a reasonable excuse. It is ordained that any persons who are elected to serve as wardens for the following year should not reject or refuse the post under the same penalty. It is ordained that all brothers and sisters and widows in their own right should pay the mass penny for any deceased brother or sister within the period of a month after the day of the funeral. Each and every one of these ordinances and agreements have been prescribed and are to be adhered to, observed in the stated form and implemented by all. In token of which, to demonstrate their faithful intentions, all the aforesaid brothers and sisters, by common assent, have in turn made their corporal oaths by touching the holy Gospels of God.

[page 8.]
Presentation of accounts on the Sunday after Christmas. The wardens of the goods of the said Fraternity came and rendered their account, namely Stephen Webbe and

Edward Hoden. They handed over 12s. to John Palmer with William Bestelawe and William Hore as his pledges and 12s. to Walter Stowre with Walter Quintayn and Henry Tyte as his pledges.

Presentation of accounts on the Sunday as above in 3 Henry VI [1424-1425]. The wardens of the said Fraternity, namely John Palmer junior and Walter Stowre, came and rendered their account, to the value of 24s. And so they handed over to the aforesaid John Palmer with William Hore and William Bestelawe as his pledges 12s.; and to Edward Howden the same sum, with John But and Richard Brangwaynger as his pledges.

Presentation of accounts on the Sunday after Christmas. The wardens of the said Fraternity, namely Edward Howdyn and John Palmer junior, came and rendered their account to the value of 24s. And so they handed it over to the store. And the wardens were elected for the next year, namely the aforesaid Edward, who received 12s. 6d. with John Hore and Roger Dowyntre as his pledges; and also John Palmer, who received 12s. with William Bestelawe and Walter Mason as his pledges. Dated 4 Henry VI [1425-1426].

[page 9]
Presentation of accounts on the Sunday after Christmas. The wardens of the said Fraternity, namely Edward Howdon and John Palmer junior, came and rendered their account to the value of 22s. And so they handed it over to the store. And the wardens were elected for the next year, namely the aforesaid Edward, who received 13s. 6d. with Roger Dowyntre and Richard Webbe as his pledges; and also John Palmer, who received 13s. 6d. with William Bestelawe and Thomas Mankyswyl as his pledges. Dated 5 Henry VI [1426-1427].

Presentation of accounts on the Sunday after Christmas. The wardens of the goods of the said Fraternity, namely Edward Houdon and John Palmer junior, came and rendered their account to the value of 20s 8d. And so they handed it over to the store. And the wardens were elected for the next year, namely the aforesaid Edward, who received 14s. with Roger Dowyntre and Richard Webbe as his pledges; and also John Palmer junior, who received 14s. with William Bestelawe and Thomas Mankeswill as his pledges. Dated 7 Henry VI [1428-1429, *presumably a mistake for the 6th year, see entries before and after*].

[page 10]
Presentation of accounts on the Sunday after Christmas. The wardens of the goods of the said Fraternity, namely Edward Houdon and John Palmer junior, came and rendered their account to the value of 28s. And they handed it over to the store. And the wardens were elected for the next year, namely the aforesaid Edward who received 15s. 6d. with Roger Dowyntre and John Hoor as his pledges; and also John Palmer junior, who received 15s. 6d. with William Bestelawe and Thomas Mankeswill as his pledges. Dated 7 Henry VI [1428-1429]. Total 31s.

Presentation of accounts on the Sunday after Christmas. The wardens of the goods of the said Fraternity, namely Edward Houden and John Palmer junior, came and rendered their account to the value of 31s. And the wardens were elected for the next year, namely Edward Houden, who received 15s. 6d. with John Prout and Walter Mason as his pledges; and also John Palmer junior, who received 15s. 6d. with John But and Thomas Mankeswill as his pledges. Dated 8 Henry VI [1429-1430].

[page 11]
Presentation of accounts on the Sunday after Christmas. The wardens of the goods of the said Fraternity, namely Edward Howden and John Palmer, came and rendered their account to the value of 31s. And the wardens were elected for the next year, namely Edward Howden, who received 15s. 6d. with Walter Mason and Roger Dawynter as his pledges; and also John Palmer junior, who received 15s. 6d. with Thomas Mankeswill and John Butt as his pledges. Dated 9 Henry VI [1430-1431].

Presentation of accounts on the Sunday after Christmas. The wardens of the goods of the said Fraternity came and rendered their account to the value of 31s. And they elected wardens for the next year, namely Edward Howden with Stephen Webbe and John Ovyet as his pledges; and also John Palmer junior with John But and John Pyres as his pledges. And each of these wardens received 15s. 6d. Dated 10 Henry VI [1431-1432]. Total 31s.

Presentation of accounts on the Sunday after Christmas. The wardens of the said Fraternity came and rendered their account to the value of 31s. And they elected wardens for the next year, namely Edward Howden with Walter Mason and Roger Dowyntre as his pledges; and also John Palmer junior with Thomas Mankeswill and John Mankeswill as his pledges. And each of these wardens received 15s. 6d. Dated 11 Henry VI [1432-1433]. [Total] 31s.

[page 12]
Presentation of accounts on the Sunday after Christmas. The wardens of the said Fraternity came and rendered their account to the value of 31s. And they elected wardens for the next year, namely John Peers with John Hore and Richard Brangwayne as his pledges; and also Stephen Webbe with Edward Saundres and John Borage as his pledges. And each of these wardens received 15s. 6d. Dated 12 Henry VI [1433-1434]. Total 31s.

Presentation of accounts on the Sunday after Christmas. The wardens of the said Fraternity came and rendered their account to the value of 31s. 10d. And they elected wardens for the next year, namely John Peeris with Richard Brangwayn and Walter Quintayne as his pledges; and also Stephen Webbe senior with John Brode and John Butte as his pledges. And each of these wardens received 13s. 4d. And the remainder they handed over to the upper room of the community [*Et relictum tradiderunt ad solarium c[ommunita]tis*] Dated 13 Henry VI [1434-1435]. Total 31s. 10d.

Presentation of accounts on the Sunday after Christmas. The wardens of the said Fraternity came and rendered their account to the value of 31s. 10d. And they elected wardens for the next year, John Borage with John Brode and Edward Houdon as his pledges; and also Richard Webbe with John Palmer and Stephen Webbe as his pledges. And each of these wardens received 16s. 7d. Dated 14 Henry VI [1435-1436]. Total 33s. 2d.

[page 13]
Presentation of accounts on the Sunday after Christmas. The wardens of the said Fraternity came and rendered their account to the value of 30s. And they elected wardens for the next year, namely John Borage with John Brode and Walter Mason as his pledges; and also Richard Webbe with John Palmer and Stephen Webbe senior as his pledges. And each of these wardens received 15s. Dated 15 Henry VI [1436-1437].

Presentation of accounts on the Sunday after Christmas. The wardens of the said Fraternity came and rendered their account to the value of 30s. And they elected wardens for the next year, namely Richard Brangwayn with John Burgeys and Peter Alchyn as his pledges; and also William House with Roger Dowentre and Thomas Mankeswyll as his pledges. And each of these wardens received 15s. Total 30s.

Presentation of accounts on the Sunday after Christmas. The wardens of the said Fraternity came and rendered their account to the value of 30s. And they elected wardens for the next year, namely John Chydyok with Richard Brangwayn and Thomas Mankeswill as his pledges; and also William Howse with John Burges and John Alchyn as his pledges. And each of these wardens received 15s. Total 30s.

[page 14]
Presentation of accounts on the Sunday after Christmas. The wardens of the said Fraternity came and rendered their account to the value of 30s. And they elected wardens for the next year, namely William Howse with John Alchyn and John Palmer junior as his pledges; and also John Chydyok with John Mankeswill and Edward Howdon as his pledges. And each of these wardens received 15s. Total 30s.

Presentation of accounts on the Sunday after Christmas. The wardens of the said Fraternity came and rendered their account to the value of 30s. And they elected wardens for the next year, namely William Howse with John Burges and John Palmer junior as his pledges; and also John Chydyok with Edward Howden and John Brode as his pledges. And each of these wardens received 15s. Total 30s.

[page 15]
Presentation of accounts on the Sunday after Christmas. The wardens of the said Fraternity came and rendered their account to the value of 30s. And they elected wardens for the next year, namely William Howse with John Burges and John Palmer

junior as his pledges; and also John Chydyok with John Brode and Edward Howden as his pledges. And each of these wardens received 15s. Total 30s

Presentation of accounts on the Sunday after Christmas. The wardens of the said Fraternity came and rendered their account to the value of 30s. And they elected wardens for the next year, namely William Howse with John Burges and John Palmer junior as his pledges; and also [*name erased*] John Chydyok with John Brode and Edward Howden as his pledges. And each of these wardens received 15s. 6d. Total 31s.

[page 16]
Presentation of accounts on the Sunday after Christmas in the year of Our Lord 1442. The wardens of the said Fraternity came and rendered their account to the value of 30s. And they elected wardens for the next year, namely John Nything with John Pyrys and John Burges as his pledges; and also John Brode with John Chydyock and Edward Howden as his pledges. And each of these wardens received 15s. 6d. through the aforesaid pledges. Total 31s.

Presentation of accounts on the Sunday after Christmas in the year of Our Lord 1443. The aforesaid wardens came with their aforesaid pledges with their money received as above and acted throughout as in the following year.

~~Presentation of accounts on the Sunday after Christmas in the year of Our Lord 1444. The aforesaid wardens , that is to say John Nithyng through his pledges John Pyrys and John Burges and John Brode through the pledges of John Chydeocke and Edward Howden, came.~~

Presentation of accounts on the Sunday after Christmas in the year of Our Lord 1444. The wardens, John Nithyng through his pledges John Pyres and John Burges and John Mankeswyll through the pledges of John Chydeocke and John Brode, came. And each of the said wardens received on the said day 15s. 6d. through their aforesaid pledges. Total 31s.

[page 17]
Presentation of accounts on the Sunday after Christmas in the year of Our Lord 1445. The wardens came as above and faithfully rendered their account and elected new wardens, John Nythyng through his pledges, John Pyrys and John Brode; William Howse through his pledges John Burgess and John Palmer. And each of the said wardens received 15s. 6d. Total 26s.

Presentation of accounts on the Sunday after Christmas in the year of Our Lord 1446. The said wardens came, namely Warden John Nythyng through his pledges, that is John Pyrys and John Brode; and the other Warden, William Howse through his pledges John Burgess and John Palmer. And each of the said wardens, that is Warden John Nythyng and Warden William Howse, received 15s. 6d. Total 26s.

Presentation of accounts on the Sunday as above in the year of Our Lord 1447. The said wardens came, namely John Nythyng through his pledges, John Pyrys and John Brode; William Howse through his pledges John Burgess and John Palmer. As above. And each of the said wardens, that is Warden John Nythyng and Warden William Howse, received 15s. 6d. Total 26s.

[page 18]
Presentation of accounts on the Sunday after Christmas in the year of Our Lord 1448. The said wardens came, John Nythyng through his pledges, John Pyres and John Brode; and also William Howse the other warden with his pledges John Burgess and John Palmer. As above. And each of the said wardens received for himself 15s. 6d. Total received 26s.

Presentation of accounts on the Sunday after Christmas in the year of Our Lord 1451. The said wardens came, John Nythyng through his pledges, John Pyres and John Brode; and William Howse, the other Warden, with his pledges John Burgess and John Palmer. And they rendered their account well and faithfully concerning the aforesaid sum. And they elected new wardens, namely Edward Saundres through his pledges John Palmer and John Pyres and the other Warden John Oyet through his pledges John Brode and John Dunne.
And each of the said wardens received for himself 15s. 9d. Total 31s. 6d.

~~Presentation of accounts on the Sunday after Christmas in the year of Our Lord 1452. In 31 Henry VI, the said wardens came, namely John Palmer through his pledges John Perys and William Huse and the other Warden namely John Down through his, John Brode and Edward Howdon. And each of the said wardens received for himself 15s. 9d. Total 31s. 6d.~~

[page 19]
Presentation of accounts on the Sunday after the feast of Saint Thomas the Martyr [29 December] 31 Henry VI [1452]; the said wardens came, namely Edward Saundres through his pledges, John Palmer, and the other Warden John Oyet and they rendered their account well and faithfully concerning the aforesaid sum. And they elected new wardens, namely John Palmer through his pledges John Perys and William Huse and the other Warden namely John Down through his pledges John Brode and Edward Howden. And each of the said wardens received for himself 16s. 4d. Total 32s. 8d.

Presentation of accounts on the Sunday after the feast of Saint Thomas the Martyr in 32 Henry VI [1453]; John Palmer came through his pledges John Perys and William House and the other Warden namely John Dun through his pledges John Brode and Edward Howedon. And they rendered their account well and faithfully concerning the aforesaid sum. And they elected again the same John Palmer and John Dun through the aforesaid pledges. And each of the said wardens received for himself 16s. 4d. Total 32s. 8d.

Presentation of accounts on the Sunday after Christmas in 33 Henry VI [1454].
John Palmer and John Dun, wardens of the said Fraternity, came and rendered their
account. And they elected new wardens for the next year namely John Atkyn through
the pledges of John Nythyng and Edward Howden; and William House through the
pledges of John Burges and Robert But; these wardens received in turn 32s. from
which 8s. was accepted and handed over to William Olyver for the purchase of 2
antiphonals, that is to say ledgers, for the use of the church of St. Mary of Bridport.
And so there remains in the hands of the aforesaid wardens 24s.

[page 20]
Presentation of accounts on the Sunday after Christmas in 34 Henry VI [1455]. John
Atkyn and William Howse, wardens of the said Fraternity, came and rendered their
account. And they elected new wardens for the next year namely John Atkyn through
the pledges of John Hamell and Edward Howden; and William House through the
pledges of John Palmer and John Burges. And each of those wardens received 12s.
Total 24s. And the aforesaid wardens received 1 lb of wax from Thomas Bayley. And
Robert Skarlet received from William Olyver 8s. which William Olyver received for
purchasing 2 antiphonals for the use of the church of the Blessed Mary.

Presentation of accounts on the Sunday after Christmas in 35 Henry VI [1456].
William Howse and Margaret, widow of John Atkyn, wardens of the said Fraternity,
came and rendered their account. And they elected new wardens for the next year,
namely William Howse through the pledges of John Burges and Edward Howden;
and Margaret, widow of John Atkyn, through the pledges of John Nythyng and John
Palmer. And each of those wardens received 12s. Total 24s. And the aforesaid wardens
received 1 lb of wax from Thomas Bayley. And Robert Skarlet received from William
Olyver 8s. for purchasing 2 antiphonals for the use of the church of the Blessed Mary.

[page 21]
Presentation of accounts on the Sunday after Christmas in 37 Henry VI [1458].
William Howse and Margaret, widow of John Atkyn, wardens of the said Fraternity,
came and rendered their account. And they elected new wardens for the next year,
namely William Howse through the pledges of John Burges and Edward Howden;
and Margaret, widow of John Atkyn, through the pledges of John Nythyng and John
Palmer. And each of those wardens received 12s. Total 24s.

Presentation of accounts on the Sunday after Christmas in 38 Henry VI [1459].
William Howse and Margaret, widow of John Attekyn, wardens of the said Fraternity,
came and rendered their account. And they elected new wardens for the next year,
namely William Howse through the pledges of John Burgys and Edward Howden; and
Margaret Attekyn, through the pledges of John Nythyng and John Palmer. And each
of those wardens received 12s. Total 24s. Item: he shall receive from Nicholas Yung
half a pound of wax. Item he shall receive from Thomas Bayly 1 lb of wax.

[page 22]

Presentation of accounts on the Sunday after Christmas in 39 Henry VI [1460]. William Howse and Margaret Atkyn, widow of John Atkyn, wardens of the said Fraternity, came and rendered their account. And they elected the same wardens for the next year, namely William Howse through the pledges of John Burges and Edward Howden; and Margaret Atkyn, through the pledges of John Nythyng and [Blank, space for a name]. And each of those wardens received 12s. Total 24s.

Presentation of accounts on the Sunday after Christmas in 1 Edward IV [1461]. William Howse and Margaret Atkyn, widow of John Attekyn, wardens of the said Fraternity, came and rendered their account. And they elected new wardens for the next year, namely William Howse through the pledges of John Burgys and Edward Howden; and John Nythyng [*John Nythyng* inserted in margin], through the pledges of Margaret Atkyn and William Howse. And each of those wardens received 12s. Total 24s.

**CD12.** *Two title deeds relating to the Fraternity of the Mortuary Lights in St Mary's, 1333, exact duplicates, CD12a is damaged and torn.*

**CD12b** *Title deed relating to the Fraternity of the Mortuary Lights in St Mary's, 1333*
Let it be known to all that we, William de Larkepathe and William Colt, wardens of the lands and rents belonging to the mortuary lights of the Church of the Blessed Virgin Mary of Bridport, have handed over and conceded to Adam de Larkestoke and Alice his wife all that piece of land which is situated in the South Street of the town of Bridport on the western side between the land of Adam de Larkestoke on the western side and the curtilage of Richard Seymor to the east in width, and the land formerly belonging to Walter Hyderward to the north and the lane called La Blindelane to the south in length. To have and to hold all the said piece of land with all its appurtenances to the aforesaid Adam and Alice for the whole of their lives or the life of the one who lives longest, from us and our successors, freely, quietly, well and in peace. Paying from it annually to us and our successors two shillings and eight pence of legal money at the four principal terms in equal instalments for all manner of obligatory services and demands. And we, the aforesaid wardens and all our successors shall warrant all the aforesaid piece of land with its appurtenances to the aforesaid Adam and Alice his wife as long as they shall live (or the one who lives longest shall live), against all mortals and defend it, as said before.
To this agreement, therefore, which is to be faithfully observed by both parties, we have arranged for the seal of the community of Bridport to be attached to the part which will remain with the aforesaid Adam and Alice, and he, the said Adam for himself and Alice, has attached his seal to the parts which will remain with us. With the following witnesses: William Quarell, John known as Snaw, the bailiffs at the time. Edward Rebe, William Binne [or perhaps 'Bume'], Peter Prest, Laurence Elyoth, Peter Cukeroyl, and others. Dated at Bridport on the next Monday after the Feast of St Michael, in full court, 7 Edward III [1333].

**CD13** *Title deed relating to the Fraternity of the Mortuary Lights in St Mary's, 1342.*

To all Christ's faithful to whom this present writing shall come, Nicholas de Chideoc sends greetings in the Lord. Know that I have inspected and reviewed a certain document of John Gervays my father, in these words: Let all men present and future know that I, John Gervays have conceded to the wardens of the Lights of the Church of Saint Mary of Bridport two shillings of annual rent, arising from my tenement in Bridport situated in West Street to the north of that street between my tenement to the east and Adam Ramesham's tenement to the west. To have and to hold annually the aforesaid rent of two shillings at the four principal terms in equal instalments, freely, quietly, well and in peace to the aforesaid wardens and their successors for ever. I have also conceded to the said wardens and their successors that if the said rent of two shillings should be in arrears at any of the aforesaid terms, in part or in whole, then it will be permissible to the same wardens and their successors to enter the said tenement and make a distraint of goods there, keeping the  goods distrained to the point where the arrears of the said rent will have been settled. In testimony of which I have affixd my seal to the present document. With the following witnesses: Master John Cute, Thomas de la Grave, Richard Rothoni, Walter Drake, Richard Ramesham, and others.

Which document I, the aforesaid Nicholas de Chideoc, do confirm and ratify through the present document, asserting that whatever my father John Gervays did and conceded in regard to these above-mentioned matters is fully approved. With the following witnesses: William Quarel, Thomas Dannur bailiffs at the time, William Binne (or Bume), Edward atte Stone, William Colt, Adam Pistor, Adam Golofre, Richard Lannerans [this word is divided over two lines and may be an error for 'Laurans'], and others. Dated at Bridport on the Monday after the Feast of the Lord's Epiphany, 16 Edward III [1342].

**CD14** *A small book relating to the Fraternity of St Nicholas, covering the period 1423 to 1437. At the back of the book are a fragment of a sermon and a will, neither of which seem to relate directly to the Fraternity - see Introduction, section 5.4.*

[page 1]
These are the names of the Brothers and Sisters of the Fraternity of St. Nicholas in the church of the Blessed Mary of Bridport:

William Bowley [and] Cristina his wife
John Mustard
Walter Quynteyne  Agnes his wife
William Mylwarde and his wife Joan
William Parnam and his wife Lettice
John Hoore and his wife Joan
John Sterre and his wife Lucy
William Marchal and his wife Joan
William Butt and his wife Ammota

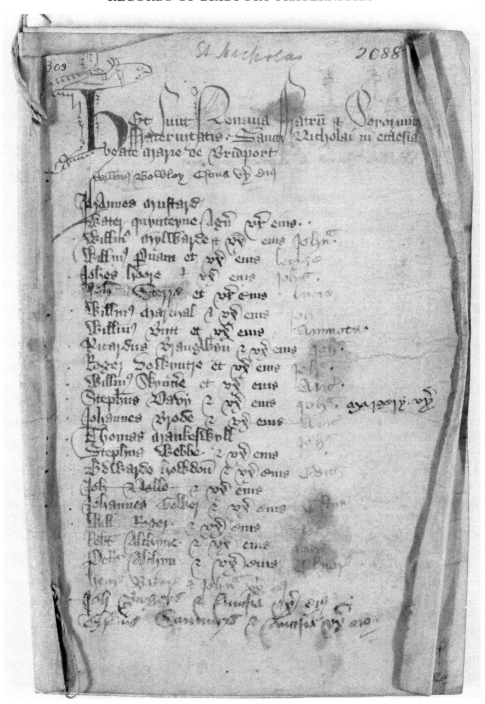

*The first page of DC-BTB/CD/14 names of the members of the Fraternity of St Nicholas*

Richard Brangwyn and his wife Joan
Roger Dowyntre and his wife Joan
William Skynnere and his wife Alice
Stephen Davy and his wife Joan, Margery wife
John Brode and his wife Alice
Thomas Mankeswyll
Stephen Webbe and his wife Joan
Edward Howdon and his wife Edith
John Dolle and his wife
John Gower and his wife Cristina
William Roger and his wife Alice
Robert Alchyne and his wife Joan
Peter Alchyn and his wife Elinor
Henry Baker and Joan his wife
John Burgeys and Amisia his wife
Thomas Symmys and Amisia his wife

[page 2]
Robert Hayvyle and his wife Isabel
William Walter and his wife Cristina
Thomas Bakere and his wife
William Lane and Agnes his wife

[page 3] (*The ordinances or rules of the Fraternity*)
It has been has been ordained and agreed between the aforesaid brothers and sisters
by common assent as follows: that each brother or sister should come annually to give
a faithful hearing to the reading of the accounts, that is to say on the day of the Holy
Innocent(s) after the feast of the Nativity of our Lord Jesus Christ at a suitable place
agreed by the wardens of the said Fraternity. And if any of the aforesaid brothers or
sisters should abstain from or keep away from the meeting, he or she should pay half a
pound of wax. It is also agreed and ordained that all brothers and sisters should come
to the Mass on the day of the burial of any deceased brother or sister and that they
should make an offering with them, the above penalty to be applied in the absence
of a reasonable excuse. It is ordained that any persons who are elected to serve as
wardens for the following year should not refuse the post under the same penalty. It
is ordained that all brothers and sisters and widows in their own right should pay the
mass penny for any deceased brother or sister within the period of four weeks after
the day of the funeral.

Each and every one of these ordinances have been prescribed and are to be faithfully
adhered to in the aforesaid manner. In token of which, to demonstrate their faithful
intentions, all the aforesaid brothers and sisters, by common assent, have in turn
made their corporal oaths which shall last for all time, by touching the holy Gospels
of God.

It is ordained, with the common agreement of the brothers and sisters, that if any brother or sister of the said Fraternity presumes to sell, grant or bequeath to anyone the place (literally "seat", *sedem suam*) which has been granted or allocated to him or her, the said brothers will be entitled to sell that place to any honest person acceptable to them, to the profit of the light of the said Fraternity, under the penalty of 20d., and to the profit of the promotion of the light, notwithstanding any obstacle.

[page 4]
It is ordained that if any brother or sister of the said Fraternity should depart from the light or be killed by any other misfortune, and his body can be found, within the distance of three miles, then the body should be brought by the brothers to the nearest and most convenient place where it can be buried, at the expense of that deceased brother or sister, if they have enough of their own money; if not, at the expense of the said Fraternity.

It is ordained that if any brother or sister of the aforesaid Fraternity should come to such poverty that they are unable to maintain themselves from their own resources, then he or she should receive from each member of the Fraternity one penny per month, through the wardens of the said Fraternity, until he or she recovers from their poverty.

It is to be remembered that on the Day of the Innocents 2 Henry VI [1423] Walter Quyntin and Edward Haudon, wardens of the goods of the Fraternity of St Nicholas of Bridport, [came] and each of them received 14s. from the funds of the aforesaid Fraternity and the aforesaid Walter received 14s. 4d. through the pledge of William Mylword. And Edward Howdon received the same sum through the pledge of William Parnam.

It is to be remembered that on the Day of the Innocents 4 Henry VI [1425] Walter Quynteyn and Edward Hodyn, wardens of the goods of the Fraternity of St Nicholas of Bridport came, and the aforesaid Walter received 14s. through the pledge of William Milword and Edward Hodyn received 14s. through the pledge of William Parnam.

[page 5]
It is to be remembered that on the Day of the Innocents in the [*year missing*] year of King Henry VI Walter Quynteyn and Edward Howdon, wardens of the goods of the Fraternity of St Nicholas of Bridport [came], and the aforesaid Walter received 14s. through the pledges of Richard Brandwyne and John Brode; and Edward Howdon received 14s. through the pledges of William Walters and William Parnam.

It is to be remembered that on the Day of the Innocents 7 Henry VI [1428] Walter Quintyn and Edward Houdon, wardens of the goods of the Fraternity of St Nicholas of Bridport (came), and the aforesaid Walter received 16s. 6d. And Edward Haudon received 16s. 6d. through the pledges of Richard Brangwyne and John Brode; and

Edward Haudon received 15s. 6d. through the pledges of William Walters and John Hore.

It is to be remembered that on the Day of the Innocents 7 Henry VI [1428] Walter Quynteyn and Edward Howden, wardens of the goods of the Fraternity of St Nicholas of Bridport [came] and rendered their account, namely 32s. and new wardens were elected namely William Walterys and he received 14s. 4d. through the pledges of John Borage and Walter Quynteyn; and William Mylward and he received 14s. 4d. through the pledges of William Parnam and John Brode.
Total 28s. 8d. [*signed with two marks*]

[page 6]
It is to be remembered that on the day of the Circumcision 8 Henry VI [1429] William Bouley and William Mylward, wardens of the Fraternity of the Light of St. Nicholas came and paid to the store 28s. 8d. and new wardens were elected, ~~William~~ Walter Mason and he received through the pledges of William Bouley and Richard Brangwayne and he received 14s. 4d.; and Stephen Davy received 14s. 4d. through the pledges of John Burgeys and John Brode.
Total 28s. 8d.

It is to be remembered that on the day of the Circumcision 9 Henry VI [1430] Walter Mason and Stephen Davy, wardens of the Fraternity of the Light of St. Nicholas came and they elected Walter Mason through the pledges of William Bowley and Richard Brangwayne; and Stephen Davy through the pledges of John Borage and John Brode. And each of these wardens received 14s. 4d.
Total 28s. 8d.

It is to be remembered that on the day of the Innocents 10 Henry VI [1431] Walter Mason and Stephen Davy, wardens of the Fraternity of the Light of St. Nicholas came and paid to the store 28s. 8d. And the brothers elected Walter Mason through the pledges of William Bowley and Richard Brangwayn; and Stephen Davy through the pledges of John But and Thomas Mankeswill. And each of these wardens received 14s. 4d.
Total 28s. 8d.

[page 7]
It is to be remembered that on the day of the Innocents 11 Henry VI [1432] Walter Mason and Stephen Davy, wardens of the Fraternity of the Light of St. Nicholas of Bridport came and paid to the store 28s. And the brothers elected Walter Mason through the pledges of William Bouley and William Marchall; and Stephen Davy through the pledges of Thomas Mankeswill and William Skinner. And each of these wardens received 14s. 4d.
Total 28s. 8d.

It is to be remembered that on the day of the Innocents 12 Henry VI [1433], Walter Mason and Stephen Davy, wardens of the Fraternity of the Light of St. Nicholas of

Bridport came and rendered their account. And they elected new wardens for the next year, namely Walter Mason through the pledges of William Bowley and William Marchall; and Stephen Davy through the pledges of Richard Webbe and Thomas Symmys. And each of these wardens received 14s. 8d. Total 29s. 4d.

It is to be remembered that on the day of the Innocents 13 Henry VI [1434] Walter Mason and Stephen Davy, wardens of the Fraternity of the Light of St. Nicholas of Bridport came and rendered their account. And they elected wardens for the next year, namely Walter Mason through the pledges of William Bowley and John Burges; and Stephen Davy through the pledges of Richard Brangewayne and Thomas Symmys. And each of these wardens received 14s. 8d.
Total 29s. 4d.

[page 8]
It is to be remembered that on the day of the Innocents 14 Henry VI [1435] Walter Mason and Stephen Davy, wardens of the Fraternity of the Light of St. Nicholas of Bridport came and rendered their account. And they elected wardens for the next year, namely Stephen Davy through the pledges of John Burges and John But; and Thomas Symmys through the pledges of John Sterre and Thomas Mankeswyll. And each of these wardens received 14s. 8d.
Total 29s. 4d.

It is to be remembered that on the day of the Innocents 15 Henry VI [1436] Stephen Davy and Thomas Symmys, wardens of the Fraternity of the Light of St. Nicholas of Bridport came and rendered their account. And they elected wardens for the next year, namely Thomas Mankyswill through the pledges of William March and Stephen Davy; and Edward Howdon through the pledges of John Butte and Stephen Webbe. And each of these wardens received 14s. 8d.
Total 29s. 4d.

It is to be remembered that on the day of the Innocents 16 Henry VI [1437] Thomas Mankeswill and Edward Howdon, wardens of the Fraternity of the Light of St. Nicholas of Bridport came and rendered their account. And they elected new wardens for the next year, namely John Gower through the pledges of William Bowley and Richard Brangwayn; and John Brode through the pledges of John Burgeys and William Bowley. And each of these wardens received 14s. 8d. Total 29s. 4d.

[page 9, *inserted at end of the volume, any link to the Fraternity is unclear*]

[Latin] Well done, thou good and faithful servant  Well done, good servant   (Matt 25 v21)

[English] (*the character yogh has been represented by the character ȝ, thorn has been represented by the character þ*)

Les[er] leve s[er]dg at þe by gynnyng of þ[i]s short collacio[n] þe whiche I be þe grace of god p[ro]pos to saye at þ[i]s tyme I be sheche ʒow at þis tyme to helpe me w[i]t[h] ʒowr holy prayers þ[a]t y may be abule to saye su[m] gode word thyʒfe þe [con]fermaci[on] of the holy gost þ[a]t hyt may be profetabul & salvaci[o]n un to yowr saulys & myne allso whene we schal take þe waye of alle mo[n]ne kynded to anoder word *(sic)* þ[a]t as ys boþe ~~goe~~ yoe(?) & blys w[i]t[h] oute e[n]de Ame[n].

Gode fre[n]dis at þe by gy[n]nyng of þ[i]s short collacio[n] y reco[m]me[n]de u[n]to yowr holy prayerse all þe state of *(line with words erased)* alle holy chorche & alle so alle þe state of te[m]p[er]alte to þe heyest & to þe louest of lore(?) partyys syrytuall and te[m]p[er]al þ[a]t god of hys sovere[n] grace set th[er]ynne  suche stedefast wytte þ[a]t þe srytyallete may so teche & prece & ther[e] levyng so to schewed warkynke þ[a]t þe te[m]p[er]all[e]te may have schache laterance lygtyng to lede alle ~~all~~ krysty[n] pepull to xx ever lestyng yoder w[i]t[h] oute endyng and herto y pray all[e] a pat[er] nost[er] and ava my defoudtely sayying
Euge serve et ut supra
~~Le[ser] leve fre[n]d[is] at þe by gy[n]nyng~~

[page 10]  (*The will of Robert Pewterer*)
In the name of God, on 21 August 1451, I, Robert Pewterer, being of sound mind and good memory, make my will in this way. Firstly I leave my soul to Almighty God and my body to be buried in the graveyard of the Blessed Mary, Bridport. Next I leave 8d. to the Rector of the same church. Next I leave 4d. to the Parish Clerk of the same church. Next I leave 4d. to each of my children. Next I leave 6d. to the Fabric Fund of the Church of Salisbury. Next I leave to my sister Joan a brass pot with a pan (*unam ollam eneam cum una patella*). Next I leave to my uncle of Wareham a sword with a dagger (*unum gladium cum uno dagger*). Next I leave to my uncle sir Robert a maple wood bowl and a dish (*unam murram cum una cratera*). Next I leave to the same uncle a silver belt (*zonam argenteam*).  And the residue of all my goods not specifically bequeathed I leave to my well-beloved [wife] in order that she can dispose of them for the sake of my soul in the best way she can determine.
[*The bottom of the page is covered with doodles and practice letters*]

[page 11]
Amen I say to you, above all things

**CD15** *A small book relating to the Fraternity of the Torches, covering period 1425 to 1461. The front and back covers are of parchment recycled from a manuscript of church music, not directly relating to the Fraternity - see Introduction, section 6.2*

[Page 3]  These are the names of the brothers and sisters of the Fraternity of the Torches, which was ordained and begun between the same brothers in the church of the Blessed Mary of Bridport on Palm Sunday AD 1421, for the purpose of maintaining candles in the torches of the aforementioned church, to the honour of our Lord Christ and his most devout mother Mary and all the Saints, that is to say:

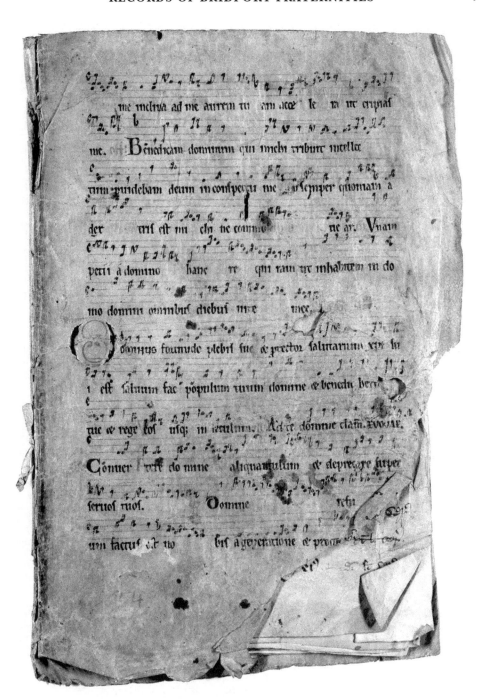

*DC-BTB/CD/15 Outer front cover*

*DC-BTB/CD/15 Inner front cover*

John Helyer, rector of Bridport church
+ Sir John Mustard
+ Sir Walter Bexington
+ Sir Robert Gylys
+ Henry Tyte, Alice his wife
+ Robert Abbot
+ Thomas at Forde, Agnes his wife
+ William Offley, ~~Alice his wife~~, Joan his wife half a pound of wax
~~Robert Lankill, Joan his wife~~ half a pound of wax
John Do, Christine his wife
Alexander Cock
William Clenche
~~Wymarke widow~~
+ Richard Threder, Agnes his wife
+ John Prior, Agnes his wife
+ Richard Deighr, Katherine his wife
+ Robert Burges, Alice his wife
+ John Crulle, Isabel his wife, qt. Isabel
+ John Pitman, Joan his wife
~~Richard Chester~~ and Helen his wife
~~Thomas Deycoke  Alice his wife~~, half a pound of wax
+ Joan Hemyok widow, half pound of wax
William Portesham, Matilda his wife, half a pound of wax

[page 4]
John at Hyde, half a pound of wax
+ Walter Saunder, Christine his wife
+ John Parrok, Joan his wife qt
William Pernham, Lettice his wife, half a pound of wax
John Gylis, ~~Alice his wife~~ and Matilda his wife
John Brode, ~~Alice~~ Margaret his wife
+ Richard Davell, Edith his wife, qt Margaret his wife
Nicholas Barbor, Joan his wife
~~Agnes Dol~~
Agnes Brekefast, half a pound of wax
Joan Gamelyn
~~Peter Alchyn and Eleanor his wife~~
John Ber and his wife Joan ~~half a pound of wax~~, a quarter of wheat
+ William Skynner and Alice his wife qt
John Hyrdeley and Alice his wife
Harry Baker, Joan his wife Agnes his wife, half a pound of wax
Gowse Palmer
Joan Coukys, half a pound of wax
William Marchal Joan his wife d+

William Ayleworth and Emmota his wife
+ Richard Cause and Joan his wife
John Leche and Alice his wife half a pound of wax
Peter Jane and Isabel his wife
William Gamelyn and Agnes his wife Katherine his wife qt
John Waterman and Isabel his wife

[page 5]
Joan Mylward formerly wife of William Mylward qt
+ Walter Warde and Joan his wife ++ qt
John James and he gave what he had to pay for four terms of the year 16d. <sup>it has been paid.</sup>
This is in the first year, then afterwards not voluntarily. And for his new wife Martina.
+ Nicholas ~~Atkynne~~ <sup>Adam</sup> and Dionisia his wife and they give for a fine in the first year
16d. <sup>it has been paid.</sup> qt
~~John Nythyng and Edith his wife and they give for a fine 16d. in payment~~
+ Thomas Bowche and Thomasina his wife and he gives for a fine ~~12d. in payment~~ qt
John Leege, because he does not want to accept the burden of the wardenship,
according to the ordinances and constitutions of the said Fraternity. Payment handed
over. That is to say 1 pound of wax
Walter Helyer, the same
John at Hydes, the same
Henry Baker, the same
Nicholas Russell [and] Agnes his wife, he will pay 12d.
+John Mayyow [and] Isabel his wife, qt, for next year, he will pay 8d. and will make
one torch
+ John Rendell [and] Emma his wife, qt, he will pay 12d.
+ John Robyns Joan his wife 12d., qt, for next year
+ John Greyston Alice [written over an erased name, perhaps *Edith*] his wife, qt, he
will pay next year
William Funtell, Agnes his wife 10d, his 12d.

[page 6]
On this day, that is to say Palm Sunday in the year of our Lord 1424 and in the third
year of the reign of King Henry VI, the former wardens came and rendered their
account for their pledges, each one for himself, and they elected new wardens with
the agreement of the whole Fraternity, namely: Richard Threder through the pledge
of Henry Tyte; Robert Burgeys through the pledge of John <sup>Brode</sup> ~~Crulle,~~ John Parrocke
through the pledge of John Crulle; and each of them for himself has 33s. 11d. in
store. And they have 188 pounds of wax in store.

On this day, that is to say Palm Sunday in the year of our Lord 1425 and 4 Henry VI,
the former wardens came and rendered their account for their pledges, each one
for himself, and they elected the former wardens again with the agreement of the
whole Fraternity, namely: Richard Threder through the pledge of Henry Tyte; Robert
Burgeys through the pledge of John Brode; John Parrocke through the pledge of

Walter Sawnder; and each of them for himself has 34s. 5d. in store. And they have 192 pounds of wax in store.

On this day, that is to say Palm Sunday in the year of our Lord 1426 and 5 Henry VI, the former wardens came and rendered their account for their pledges, each for himself, and they elected new wardens with the agreement of the whole Fraternity, Richard Threder through the pledge of William Millewarde;
[page 7]
Robert Borges through the pledge of John Brode; John Parocke through the pledge of Walter Stoure. And each of them has 34s. 5d. in store. And they have 200 pounds of wax in store.

On this day, that is to say Palm Sunday in the year of our Lord 1427 and 5 Henry VI, the former wardens came and rendered their account for their pledges, each for himself, and they elected new wardens with the agreement of the whole Fraternity, Richard Threder through the pledge of William Mylwarde; Robert Burgeyse through the pledge of John Hyrdely; John Parrok through the pledge of Walter Sawnder. And each of them for himself has 35s. in store. And they have in store 204 pounds.

On this day, that is to say Palm Sunday in the year of our Lord 1428 and 6 Henry VI, the former wardens came and rendered their account for their pledges, each for himself, and so they kept the former wardens with the agreement of the whole Fraternity, Richard Threder through the pledge of William Mylwarde, Robert Burgeyse through the pledge of John Hyrdeley, John Parroke through the pledge of Walter Sawnther, and each of them for himself has 36s. 10d and they have in store 210 pounds of wax.

On this day, that is to say Palm Sunday 7 Henry VI [1429], the former wardens came and rendered their account for their pledges, each for himself and so they kept the former wardens with the agreement of the whole Fraternity;
[page 8]
that is to say Richard Threder through the pledge of William Mylwarde, Robert Burges through the pledge of John Hyrdeley, John Parrok through the pledge of Walter Saunder and John Corle, and each of these wardens received 36s. 10d and they have in store 224 pounds of wax.

On this day, that is to say Palm Sunday 8 Henry VI [1430], the former wardens came and rendered their account for their pledges, and so they elected John Hyrdeley through the pledge of William Mylward; Robert Burges through the pledge of William Threder; Walter Saunders through the pledge of William Mylwarde, and each of these wardens received 36s. 10d and they have in store 224 pounds of wax.

[page 9]
On this day, that is to say Palm Sunday 9 Henry VI [1431], the former wardens came and rendered their account; and so they elected new wardens namely John Hyrdeley through the pledge of William Milleward and William ˢᵏʸⁿⁿᵉʳ M̶a̶r̶c̶h̶a̶l̶l̶ through the

pledge of William Marchell and Robert Burges through the pledge of William Towker alias Threder; and each of these wardens received 36s. 10d. And they have 228 pounds of wax in store.

On this day, that is to say Palm Sunday 10 Henry VI [1432], the former wardens came and rendered their account; and so they elected new wardens namely John Hyrdeley through the pledge of William Mylward and William Skynner through the pledge of William Marchell and Robert Burges through the pledge of William Towker alias Threder; and each of these wardens received 36s. 10d. And they have 228 pounds of wax in store.

On this day, that is to say Palm Sunday 11 Henry VI [1433], the former wardens came and rendered their account; and so they elected new wardens namely John Herdely through the pledge of William Mylward and Robert Burgeys through the pledge of John Brode and John Crole through the pledge of John Brode; and each of these wardens received 36s. 10d. And they have 212 pounds of wax in store.

[page 10]
On this day, that is to say Palm Sunday 12 Henry VI [1434], the former wardens came and rendered their account; and so they elected new wardens namely Robert Burgeis through the pledge of John Parocke and John Hyrdeley through the pledge of William Mylward, John Curle through the pledge of John Brode and William Skynner through the pledge of John Brode and each of them ~~have in store~~ received 27s. 6d. And each of them has 212 pounds in wax in store.

On this day, that is to say Palm Sunday 13 Henry VI [1435], the former wardens came and rendered their account; and so they elected new wardens namely Robert Burgeys through the pledge of John Parrocke and John Hyrdeley through the pledge of William Marchell, John Curle through the pledge of John Brode and William Skynner through the pledge of John Brode and each of them received 27s. 6d. And each of them has 212 pounds in wax in store.

On this day, that is to say Palm Sunday 14 Henry VI [1436], the former wardens came and rendered their account; and so they elected new wardens namely Robert Burges through the pledge ~~John Parrocke~~ and John Hyrdeley through the pledge of William Marchell, John Curle through the pledge of John Brode and Richard Cause through the pledge of William Marchell and each of them received 27s. 6d. And they have 212 pounds of wax in store.

[page 11]
On this day, that is to say Palm Sunday 15 Henry VI [1437], the aforesaid brothers came and heard the account of the wardens of the aforesaid Fraternity; and they elected new wardens for the next year namely Robert Burges through the pledge of William Gamelyn of Atlington and John Hyrdeley through the pledge of William Marchall, and John Corle through the pledge of John Brode and Richard Cawsy

through the pledge of William Marchall and each of them received 28s. 1d. And they have 212 pounds of wax in store.

On this day, that is to say Palm Sunday 16 Henry VI [1438], the aforesaid brothers came and heard the account of the wardens of the aforesaid Fraternity; and they elected new wardens for the next year namely Robert Burges through the pledge of William Gamelyn and John Hyrdeley through the pledge of William Marchall, and John Corle through the pledge of John Brode and Richard Causy through the pledge of William Marchel and each of them received 28s. 1d. And they have 212 pounds of wax in store.

[page 12]
On this day, that is to say Palm Sunday 17 Henry VI [1439], the aforesaid brothers came and heard the account of the wardens of the aforesaid Fraternity; and they elected new wardens for the next year namely William Marchell through the pledge of William Gamelyn and John Crolle through the pledge of John Brode and William Skynner through the pledge of John Parroke and Richard Davell through the pledge of John Leche and each of these wardens received 28s. 1d. And they have 212 pounds of wax in store.

On this day, that is to say Palm Sunday 18 Henry VI [1440], the aforesaid brothers came and heard the account of the wardens of the aforesaid Fraternity; and they elected new wardens for the next year namely William Marchell through the pledge of William Gamelyn and John Croll through the pledge of John Brode and William Skynner through the pledge of John Parrok and Richard Davell through the pledge of John Leche and each of these wardens received 28s. 1d. And they have 212 pounds of wax in store.

[page 13]
On this day, that is to say Palm Sunday 19 Henry VI [1441], the aforesaid brothers came and heard the account of the wardens of the aforesaid Fraternity; and they elected new wardens for the next year namely William Skynner through the pledge of Emmota But and John Croll through the pledge of John Brode and John Parroke through the pledge of William Gamelyn and Richard Davell through the pledge of John Leche and each of these wardens received 28s. 1d. And they have 212 pounds of wax in store.

And for the next year following the aforesaid date, that is to say Palm Sunday 20 Henry VI [1442], the often mentioned brothers and sisters by unanimous agreement carried out the account and elected new wardens for the following year, the aforesaid William Skynner and his pledge Walter Helyer, John Corell and his pledge John Brode, John Parrocke and his pledge William Gamelyne, Richard Davyle and his pledge John Leche; and each of these just mentioned wardens received 28s. 1d. of lawful money for the aforesaid year. And the same wardens have in store, left there from the aforesaid year, 174 pounds [of wax], that is to say in candles made in the aforesaid year.

And on this day, that is to say Palm Sunday 21 King VI [1443], the said wardens [rendered] their account for that year with the consent and agreement of the brothers and sisters of the aforesaid Fraternity, and they elected new wardens for the next year with their pledges, namely John Corell, his pledge John Brode, Richard Davyle and his pledge John Leege, John Parrock and his pledge, William Gamelyn; and each of them received into store 28s. 8d. And John Brode received into store 28s. 8d. And they have in store, in torches of the said Fraternity, 199 pounds of wax.

[page 14]
On this day, that is to say Palm Sunday 22 Henry VI [1444], the aforesaid brothers came and heard the account of the wardens of the aforesaid Fraternity; and they elected new wardens for the next year namely John Parrocke through the pledge of William Gamelyn, John Crulle through the pledge of John Brode and Richard Davell through the pledge of William Gamelyn; and each of them received 28s. And John Lech through the pledge of John Beer and Nicholas Atkyn through the pledge of John Brode; and each of them received 14s. 4d. And they have 184 pounds of wax in store.

On this day of Palms in the 3 (sic) Henry VI [1445], the aforesaid brothers came and heard the account of the wardens of the aforesaid Fraternity; and they had the wardens as above, that is to say John Parrocke through the pledge of William Gamelyn, John Crulle through the pledge of John Brode and Richard Davell through the pledge of William Gamelyn; and each of them received 25s. In addition they had as wardens John Leche through the pledge of John Beer and Nicholas Atkyn through the pledge of John Brode; and each of them received 14s. 4d. And they have 187 pounds of wax in store.

Also on this Palm day, Palm Sunday 4 (sic) Henry VI [1446], the aforesaid brothers came and carried out the account. And they elected wardens namely John Parrocke through the pledge of William Gamelyn, John Crulle through the pledge of John Brode and Richard Davelle through the pledge of William Gamelyn; and each of these wardens received for themselves 25s. Also they had as wardens John Leche through the pledge of John Beer and also Nicholas Atkyn through the pledge of John Brode; and each of them received 12s. 7½d.   6d. (sic). And they have 188 pounds of wax in store.

[page 15]
On this day, that is to say Palm Sunday 1447, the aforesaid came and heard the account of the wardens of the aforesaid Fraternity. And they elected new wardens for the next year namely John Parroke through the pledge of William Gamelyn, John Crolle through the pledge of John Brode, Richard Davelle through the pledge of William Gamelyn; and each of these wardens received for themselves 25s. 3d. Also they had as wardens John Leche through the pledge of Thomas Bowge and also Nicholas Atkyn through the pledge of John Brode; and each of these two wardens received 12s. 7½d.

And they have 189 pounds of wax in store.

On this day, that is to say Palm Sunday 1448, the aforesaid wardens came and heard the account of the wardens of the aforesaid Fraternity. And they elected new wardens for the next year namely John Parroke through the pledge of William Gamelyn, John Crolle through the pledge of John Brode, Richard Davelle through the pledge of William Gamelyn; and each of these wardens received for themselves 25s. 3d. Also
[page 16]
they had two wardens namely John Mayyow through the pledge of Thomas Bowge and also Nicholas Adam through the pledge of John Rendell; and each of these two wardens received 12s. 6d. And they have 190 pounds of wax in store.

On this day, that is to say Palm Sunday 1449, the aforesaid wardens came and heard the account of the wardens of the aforesaid Fraternity. And they elected new wardens for the next year namely John Parroke through the pledge of William Gamelyn, John Crolle through the pledge of John Brode, Richard Davelle through the pledge of William Gamelyn; and each of these wardens received 25s. 3d. Also they had two wardens namely John Mayyow through the pledge of Thomas Bowge and Nicholas Adam through the pledge of John Rendell; and each of these two wardens received 12s. 6d. And they have 190 pounds of wax in store.

[page 17]
On this day, that is to say Palm Sunday 1450, the aforesaid wardens came and heard their account, that is to say of the aforesaid Fraternity. And they elected new wardens for the next year namely John Parroke through the pledge of William Gamelyn, John Crolle through the pledge of John Brode, Richard Davell through the pledge of William Gamelyn; and each of these wardens received 25s. 3d. Also they had two wardens namely John Mayyow through the pledge of Thomas Bouge and Nicholas Adam through the pledge of John Rendell; and each of these two wardens received 13s. And they have 194 pounds of wax in store.

On this day, that is to say Palm Sunday 1451, the aforesaid wardens came and heard their account, that is to say of the aforesaid Fraternity. And they elected new wardens for the next year namely John Parrok through the pledge of William Gamelyn, Nicholas Adam through the pledge of John Rendell,
[page 18]
Richard Davell through the pledge of William Gamelyn; and each of these wardens received 25s. 3d. Also they had two wardens namely John Crull through the pledge of John Brode and John Mayyow through the pledge of Thomas Buche; and each of these two wardens received 13s. And they have 194 pounds of wax in store.

On this day, that is to say Palm Sunday 1452, the aforesaid wardens came and heard their account, that is to say of the aforesaid Fraternity. And they elected new wardens for the next year namely John Parroke through the pledge of William Gamelyn, and he received 25s. 3d.

Nicholas Adam through the pledge of    }Thomas Buche
John Mayyow through the pledge of     }
    They received 26s.
John Crolle [and] Thomas Buche through the pledge of John Greyston
    They received 25s. 3d.
Richard Davell [and] John Rendell through the pledge of John Greyston
    They received 25s. 3d.
~~and each of these six wardens received~~
And they have 194 pounds of wax in store.


[page 19]
On this day, that is to say Palm Sunday 1453, the aforesaid wardens came and heard the account, that is to say of the aforesaid Fraternity. And they elected new wardens for the next year namely:
John Parrok through the pledge of William ᶠᵘⁿᵗᵉˡˡ Gamelyn, and he received 25s. 3d.
John Crolle through the pledge of John Brode received 25s. 3d.
Nicholas Adam [and] John Mayyow through the pledge of Thomas Buche, received 26s.
Richard Davell Davell (sic) through the pledge of John Greyston received 25s. 3d.
And they have 194 pounds of wax in store.


On this day, (written above: in the house of John Mayyow) that is to say Palm Sunday 1454, the aforesaid wardens came and heard the account, that is to say of the aforesaid Fraternity. And they elected new wardens for the next year namely John Parrok through the pledge of William Funtell, and he received 25s. 3d.
John Crolle [and] John Rendell through the pledge of J Brode, received (below) 25s. 3d.
Nicholas Adam [and] John Mayyow through the pledge of Thomas Bouche, received 26s.
Richard Davell through the pledge of John Greyston received 25s. 3d.
And they have 195 pounds of wax in store.


[page 20]
On this day, in the house of John Brode and Nicholas Adam, that is to say Palm Sunday 1455, the aforesaid wardens came and heard the account, that is to say of the aforesaid Fraternity. And they elected new wardens for the next year namely John Parrok through the pledge of William Funtell, and he received 25s. 3d.
John Croll and Isabel his wife through the pledge of John Mayyow and Thomas Bowche and they received 25s. 3d.
Nicholas Adam [and] John Mayyow through the pledge of John Rendell, they received 26s.
Richard Davell through the pledge of John Greyston, he received 25s. 3d.
And they have 195 pounds of wax in store.

On this day, in the house of John Brode and Nicholas Adam, that is to say Palm Sunday 1456, the aforesaid wardens came and heard the account, that is to say of the aforesaid Fraternity. And they elected new wardens for the next year namely John Parrok through the pledge of William Funtell, and he received 25s. 3d.,

John Mayyow and Nicholas Adam through the pledge of John Rendell and they received 26s.

Richard Davell through the pledge of John Greyston and he received 25s. 3d.

John Croll and Isabel his wife through the pledge of John Mayyow and ~~Thomas Bouche~~ Nicholas Adam and they received 26s.

And they have 196 pounds of wax in store.

[page 21]
On this day, in the house of John Brode and Nicholas Adam, that is to say Palm Sunday 1457, the aforesaid wardens came and heard the account, that is to say of the aforesaid Fraternity. And they elected new wardens for the next year namely John Parrok through the pledge of William Potell, and he received 25s. 3d.,

John Mayyow and Nicholas Adam through the pledge of John Rendal and they received 26s.

Richard Davell through the pledge of John Greyston he received 25s. 3d.

John Crolle and Isabel his wife through the pledge of John Mayyow and Nicholas Adam and they received 26s.

And they have 197 pounds of wax in store.

On this day, in the house of John Mayyow, that is to say Palm Sunday 1458, the aforesaid wardens came and heard the account, that is to say of the aforesaid Fraternity. And they elected new wardens for the next year namely John Parroke through the aforesaid pledge, and he received 25s. 3d.,

John Mayyow and Nicholas Adam through the aforesaid pledge, namely John Rendall, they received 26s.

John Crolle and Isabel his wife through the pledge of John Mayyow and they received 26s.

And they have 198 pounds of wax in store.

[page 22]
Also it is ordained that, by the common assent of all the brothers and sisters of the said Fraternity, the aforesaid wardens should pay for a luncheon on the day of the accounting, three pence on bread, and three gallons of good beer.

[page 23, *parchment cover of recycled music*]
[*written below the music inside the cover*] And each of them received 28s. 6d.
And let it be noted that Nicholas Atkyn and James Baker, these brothers, were appointed.

**CD16**  A s*mall book relating to the Fraternity of the Two Torches, covering period 1419 to 1480. At the back there are what appear to be some doodles, unrelated to the Fraternity. See Introduction*

*DC-BTB/CD/15 Inner back cover*

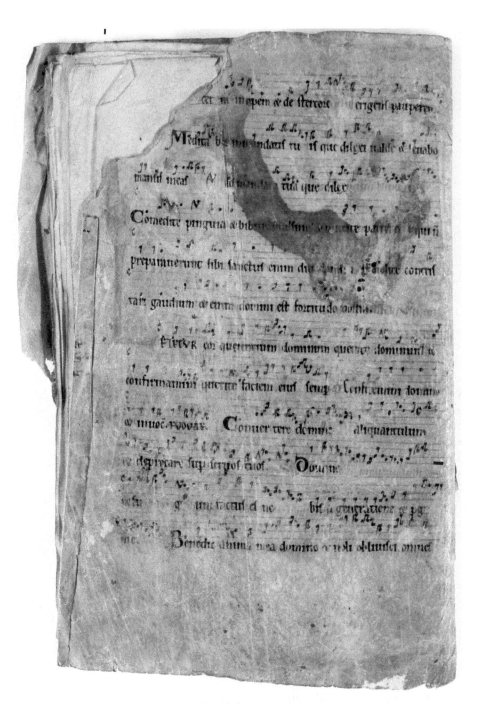

*DC-BTB/CD/15 Outer back cover*

*Section 6.2*

[page 1, *only a fragment of this page, the top right hand corner, survives*]
[ ... ] and of the sisters who are in need on the day
[ ... ] next after Easter, which
[ ... ] reasonable
[ ... ] to the great altar
[ ... ] on Sundays and other feasts
[ ... ] [and s]isters deceased of the said Fraternity
[ ... ] a penny for his soul
[ ... ] the dead person is buried. And that
[ ... ] for the soul of the deceased
[ ... ] torch is 26 lbs   *(compare CD16 p20)*

[page 2]
These are the names of the Fraternity of the Two Candles which are called "Torches":

Henry Tyte  Alice his wife
William Stowre and ~~Joan his wife~~ Isabel his wife
Walter Sawndrys and Christina his wife
+ William Helyer and Joan his wife, ½ lb wax
~~Lucy Beres~~
~~Walter Colwylle, 4d.~~
William Ovyet ~~and Alice his wife and Christiana his wife~~ Thomasia his wife
~~Alice Draper~~
John Ovyet ~~and Alice his wife~~ and Florence his wife
John Newton and Joan his wife
Edward Sawndrys and J[. *hole in paper*]
~~John Lane and Margery his wife~~ [. *hole in paper*]
~~John Homan and Amota his wife~~ [... *hole in paper*]
~~Roger Homan and Elsota  his wife~~ [... *hole in paper*]
+ John Bestelaw ~~and Agnes his wife~~ [... *hole in paper*]
+ John Nythyng and Edith [... *hole in paper*]
~~William Perys servant of Peter Alchyn~~
Nicholas Pyrs and Lucy his wife
+ Stephen Davy ~~and Joan his wife~~ Marion his wife
~~Robert Hore and Joan his wife~~
~~Nicholas Barber and Joan his wife~~

[page 3]
Robert Burgeys ~~Joan~~ and Alice his wife, ½ lb wax
John Butte and Joan his wife
~~Walter Percey and Florence his wife~~
~~William Freman~~ and Alice his wife
+ John Palmer junior and Joan his wife

John Waterman and Isabel his wife
~~Nicholas Barber and Joan his wife~~
John Haynolfe and Elena his wife
William Fontell and Agnes his wife, 2d.
~~William Swayn and Christina his wife~~
[... *hole in paper*] Agnes his wife, ~~4~~d.
[... *hole in paper*] ~~Elinor his wife~~
[... *hole in paper*] a his wife
[... *hole in paper*] ~~and Margaret his wife, ½ lb wax~~
[... *hole in paper*] servant of John Clement and Emma his wife
[... *hole in paper*] ~~ne~~
[... *hole in paper*] and Joan his wife, ½ lb wax
~~William Potelle [and] Alice his wife~~
Alice Porters ~~2d.~~ 3d.
+ John Brode and Alice his wife
~~William Dowke and Alice his wife~~
~~wife of William Dowke~~

[page 4]
+ Stephen Webbe and Eleanor his wife
Thomas Stockefysh and Agnes his wife
Thomas Newton Alice his wife
Nicholas Hore and Alice his wife, 10d
Edward Tracy and Margaret his wife, 1 lb of wax
~~+ John Algar and Lucy his wife~~
John Boleyn junior and Alice his wife, for a fine 12d.
John Sterre and Lucy his wife, for a fine 1 lb of wax
Richard Burgh and Agnes his wife, for a fine 12d. +
Richard Marchall and Margaret his wife, 1 lb of wax
William Howchyn, servant of John Hill mercer, for a fine 12d.+
John Piris and Agnes his wife and he gives for a fine 12d.
William Keche and Joan his wife and he gives for a fine 12d.
John atte Weer and Isabel his wife and he gives for a fine 12d.
+ John Bittisgate and Joan his wife and he gives for a fine 12d.
William Crocker and Edith his wife and he gives for a fine 12d.
+ Richard Orchard for a fine 1 lb of wax, paid
+ John Bremell and Alice his wife for a fine 6d., paid
+ William Wykes and Christina his wife for a fine ½ lb of wax, paid
Robert Burgh and Joan his wife for a fine 6d.
Thomas Porter and Alice his wife for a fine 6d.
Thomas Benett and Matilda his wife for a fine 6d.
John Lyllyng [blank space], for a fine 6d.

[page 5]
On the Tuesday after Easter 7 Henry V [1419], William Helier and Walter Percy,

wardens of the said Fraternity, came and rendered 53s. 3d. in store, and they elected new wardens, namely the aforesaid William Helier through the pledges of Henry Tyte and Walter Syferweste and Walter Percy through the pledges of John Hore and William Stowre, and each of them has in store 26s. 8d.

On the Tuesday after Easter 8 Henry V [1420], William Helier came with John Hore, who was the pledge of Walter Percy, wardens of the said Fraternity of the Torches, and they rendered their account, that is to say in store 56s. 4d., and they elected new wardens for the next year, namely John Palmer through the pledges of John Nythyng and John Ovyet, and William Walter through the pledges of Nicholas Peyrs and John Bulleyn, and each of them has in their custody 28s. 2d.

On the Tuesday after Easter 9 Henry V [1421], John Palmer, through the pledges of John Nithyng and John Ovyet, and William Walter, through the pledges of Nicholas Peyrys and John Bulleyn, came and rendered in store 56s. 4d. And they elected new wardens for the next year, namely Nicholas Peyrs through the pledges of Robert Hore and William Walter, and John Hore through the pledges of John Nithing and John Palmer.
[page 6]
And each of them has 25s. 7d. in his custody.

Let it be remembered that on Tuesday after Easter 1 Henry VI [1423], the brothers of the Fraternity of the Torches came and there by common assent elected as wardens of the goods of that Fraternity Stephen Davi  through the pledge of ~~Robert Whor~~ John Nythyng, and Richard Adam through the pledge of William Helyer.
And each of them received into his custody 26s. 3d.

Let it be remembered that on Tuesday after Easter 3 Henry VI [1425], the brothers of the Fraternity of the Torches came and by agreement elected as wardens of the goods of that Fraternity Stephen Davy through the pledges of Nicholas Pyrys and John Nythyng and Stephen Webbe through the pledges of Henry Tyte and William Helyer. And each of them received into his custody 27s. 3d.

Let it be remembered that on Tuesday after Easter 4 Henry VI [1426] , the brothers of the Fraternity of the Torches came and by agreement elected as wardens of the goods of that Fraternity Roger Homan, through the pledges of Henry Tyte and John Nythyng, he received 27s. 5d., and John Palmer junior through the pledges of John But and William Walter, he received the same sum into his custody, namely 27s. 5d.

[page 7]
Let it be remembered that on Tuesday after Easter 5 Henry VI [1427], the brothers of the said Fraternity of the Torches came and by agreement elected as wardens of the goods of that Fraternity John Nythyng, through the pledges of Stephen Davy and John Brode, they received 28s. 1d.,  and John Ovyet through the pledges of John But and John Bestelawe, he received the same sum into his custody, namely 28s. 1d. And

in store they have 46s. 2d. [added below:] and 10d.

Let it be remembered that on Tuesday after Easter 7 Henry VI [1427-1428], the ~~brothers~~ wardens of the said Fraternity, John Nythyng and John Ovyet came and rendered their account and they elected new wardens namely William Fontell through the pledges of William Bouley and John Brode, and William Ovyet through the pledges of John But and John Ovyet. And each of these wardens received into their custody 30s
Total Sum: £3.

Let it be remembered that on Wednesday after Easter 9 Henry VI [1430-1431], the wardens ~~of the said~~ the wardens (sic) of the said Fraternity, that is to say William Fontell and William Ovyet, came and rendered their account and they elected new wardens namely William Bowley through the pledges of John Nythyng and John Palmer junior, and John But through the pledges of Stephen Dawy and William Ovyet. And each of these wardens received into their custody 31s. 6d.
Total: £3 3s.

[page 8]
Let it be remembered that on ~~Wednesday~~ Tuesday after Holy Easter 10 Henry VI [1432], the wardens of the said Fraternity, namely William Funtell and William Ovyet, came and rendered their account and they elected new wardens namely John Nythyng through the pledges of William Bowley and John Brode, and Stephen Davy through the pledges of John But and John Palmer, and William Ovyet through the pledges of John But and John Forsey. And each of these wardens received 20s [30s.]
Total: £3.

Let it be remembered that on Tuesday after Holy Easter 13 Henry VI [1435], the wardens of the said Fraternity, namely John Nythyng, Stephen Davy and William Ovyet, came and rendered their account and they elected new wardens namely John Brode through the pledges of John Nythyng and William Bowley, William Helyer through the pledges of W Bowley and Stephen Davy, William Funtell through the pledges of John Ovyet and Thomas Stocfyssh. And each of them received 20s 7d. Total £3 21d.

Let it be remembered that on Tuesday after Holy Easter 15 Henry VI [1437], the wardens of the said Fraternity, namely John Brode, William Helyer and William Funtell, came and rendered their account and they elected new wardens for the next year namely ~~John Brode~~ John Nythyng through the pledges of ~~John Forsey~~ Stephen Davy and John Nythyng (sic), ~~William Ovyet~~); William Helyer John Bestelawe through the pledges of John But and William Bowley; and William Funtell through the pledges of William Bowley and John Ovyet.
And each of these wardens received 16s. 8d. Total: 50s.

[page 9]
Let it be remembered that on Tuesday after Holy Easter 17 Henry VI [1439], the

wardens of the said Fraternity, namely John Nythyng, William Helyer, William Funtell, came and rendered their account and they elected new wardens for the next year namely William Helyer through the pledges of William Bowley and John Brode, and William Funtell through the pledges of John Forsay and Thomas Stockfysh, and John Ovyet through the pledges of Thomas Stockefysche and John Brode. And each of these wardens received 17s. 1d.

Total Sum: 51s. 3d.

And one torch is 30lb.

Let it be remembered that on Tuesday after Holy Easter 19 Henry VI [1441], the wardens of the said Fraternity, namely William Helyer, William Funtell and John Ovyet, came and rendered their account. And they elected new wardens for the next year namely John Bestelawe through the pledges of Stephen Davy and John Nythyng, Stephen Webbe through the pledges of William Helyer and John Brode, and John Palmer through the pledges of John Ovyet and John Nythyng. And each of these wardens received 17s. 9d.

Total Sum: 53s. 3d.

[page 10]

Let it be remembered that on Tuesday after Holy Easter 21 Henry VI [1443], the wardens of the said Fraternity, namely John Bestelawe Stephen Webbe and John Palmer came and rendered their account. And they elected new wardens for the next year namely John Nythyng through the pledges of Stephen Davy and Thomas Stokfyshe, and John Bestelawe through the pledges of William Bowley and John Forsay, and John Palmer through the pledges of William Bowley and John Ovyet.

And each of these wardens received 19s. 8d.

Total 59s.

Let it be remembered that on Tuesday after Holy Easter in the twenty second third year of King Henry VI [1445], the wardens of the said Fraternity came. The wardens of the said Fraternity came (sic), namely John Bestelawe, Stephen Webbe and John Palmer, and rendered their account. And they elected new wardens for the next year, John Forsey through the pledges of John Butte and John Bestlawe, Thomas Stokkefysch through the pledges of Stephen Roper and John Palmer, and William Helyer through the pledges of the aforesaid Stephen Roper and the aforesaid John Bestlawe. And each of the said wardens received in cash 18s. 1d. 5d.

[page 11]

Let it be remembered that on Tuesday after Holy Easter 24 Henry VI [1446], the wardens of the said Fraternity, namely John Forsey, Thomas Stockfysch and William Helyer, came with their pledges, as previously named. And they rendered their account and elected wardens for the next year, namely John Forsey and his pledges John Butte and Thomas Newton, Thomas Stokkefysch and his pledges Stephen Roper and the aforesaid Thomas Newton. And the Warden William Helyer and his pledges Stephen Roper and John Ovyet. And each of the said wardens rendered for himself

received 19s. 1d.
Total Sum: 57s. 3d.

~~Let it be remembered that on Tuesday after Holy Easter 26 VI, the wardens of the said Fraternity, namely John Forsey, Thomas Stokfysch and William Helyer, came with their pledges John Palmer (sic) and rendered their account and elected new wardens~~ .........

~~Let it be remembered that on Tuesday after Holy Easter 28 Henry VI, the wardens of the said Fraternity, namely John Forsey, Thomas Stokfisch with their pledges, Stephen Davy and William Helyer with their pledges John Palmer and they rendered their account and elected wardens for the next year, namely John Forsey~~

Let it be remembered that on Tuesday after Holy Easter 28 Henry VI [1450], the wardens of the said Fraternity, namely John Forsey, Thomas Stokfysch and William Helyer, came with their pledges (as previously named) and they rendered their account and elected wardens for the next year, namely John Forsey and his pledge John Nythynge, Thomas Stokfyche ^and for a pledge Stephen Davy, and William Helyer and his pledge John Palmer.
And each of the said wardens received 19s. 6d.
Total: 58s. 6d.

[page 12]
Let it be remembered that on Tuesday after Easter 30 Henry VI [1452], the wardens of the said Fraternity, namely John Forshay, Thomas Stockefysch and William Helyer, came with their pledges (as previously named) and they rendered their account and elected new wardens for the next year, namely John Forshey through the pledge of John Nithing, Thomas Stockefysch through the pledge of Stephen Davy and William Helyer through the pledge of John Palmer. And each of the said wardens have in their custody ~~20~~ 19s. 10d.
Total: 4 marks, 6s. 2d. [i.e. 59s. 6d.]

Let it be remembered that on Tuesday after Easter 32 Henry VI [1454], the wardens of the said Fraternity, namely John Forshey, Thomas Stockefysch and William Helyer, came with their pledges, as previously named, and they rendered their account and elected new wardens for the following year, namely Stephen Davy through the pledge of Thomas Stockefysch, John Palmar through the pledge of John Forshay, Nicholas Hore through the pledge of William Helyer. And each of the said wardens have in their custody 20s 5d.
Total Sum: £3 15d.

[page 13]
Let it be remembered that on Tuesday after Easter 34 Henry VI [1456], the wardens of the said Fraternity, namely John Forsey, Thomas Stockfysch and William Helyer, came with their pledges and they rendered their account and elected new wardens for the next year, namely Thomas Stockfysch through the pledge of Richard Burgh,

John Forsey through the pledge of John Sterre, Nicholas Hoore through the pledge of William Helyer. And each of the said wardens have in their custody 20s 8d.
Total Sum: £3 2s.

Let it be remembered that on Sunday after Easter 36 Henry VI [1458], the wardens of the said Fraternity, namely John Forsey, Thomas Stockfysch and Nicholas Hore came with their pledges  and they rendered their account and elected new wardens for the following year, namely Richard Burgh ~~John Palmer~~ through the pledge of Thomas Stockfyssh, Richard Marchall through the pledge of John Palmer, Nicholas Hoore through the pledge of William Helyer. And each of them has in their custody through the aforesaid pledges 21s. 10d.
For the souls of John Forshey and Stephen Davy in which the said wardens are charged, that is to say:
Firstly, for the fine of John Boleyn junior 12d.
For the fine of John Sterre 6d.
For the fine of John Piris 12d.
For the fine of William Keche 12d.
Total 3s. 6d.
The aforesaid wardens are charged with the money for the mass for previously named 19 souls.

[page 14]
Let it be remembered that on Tuesday after Easter 38 Henry VI [1460], the wardens of the said Fraternity, namely Richard Burgh, Richard Marshall and Nicholas Hore, came with their pledges  and they rendered their account and elected new wardens for the next year, namely Richard Burgh through the pledge of Thomas Stockefysch, Nicholas Hore through the pledge of John Atweere and John Palmer for Richard Marshall through the pledge of Thomas Stockefysch. Each of these has in his custody 22s. ~~6d.~~ 10d
Total sum: £3 8s. 6d.

The said wardens were charged with the collection of a fine from John Atwere ~~5~~ 12d.
From John Sterre for a fine 1 lb of wax
From William Keche for a fine 12d.
From John Boleyne junior for a fine 12d. [Struck through by a later scribe and "nothing" inserted above].
From William Crocker for a fine 12d.
From John Attewere for a fine 12d.[*Struck through by a later scribe and "nothing" inserted above, John Longhe 6d, inserted and struck through*].
From Elisha [*Eliseo*] Payer for his fine 12d.[*Struck through by a later scribe, "nothing" inserted above and "doubtful" in the margin, "Thomas Benet 6d", inserted and struck through*].
~~William Wyke and Cristina his wife for their fine ½ lb of wax~~ [*inserted in the same hand as above*]
They were charged with collecting one mass penny for the souls of William Funtell and Margaret Tracy.

*[From this point the hand that made the insertions above continues the text]*
~~Richard Orchard paid one pound of wax for a fine~~
~~John Lyllyng paid 6d. for a fine~~
~~Robert Burgh for a fine 1 lb of wax~~
~~Thomas Porter for a fine 1 lb of wax~~
~~John Breman  for a fine 1 lb of wax~~

Let it be remembered that on Wednesday after Easter 6 Edward IV [1466] the wardens of the said Fraternity, namely Richard Burgh, Richard Orchard, for Nicholas Hore, came with their pledges and they rendered their account and elected new wardens for the next year, namely Richard Burgh through the pledge of Robert Burgh, Thomas Stockfysch through the pledge of John Sterre, Richard Orchard through the pledge of Thomas Porter. Each of them has in his custody 16s. 8d.
Total ~~54s. 6d.~~  ~~49s. 10d.~~ 50s. 1d.
In addition they were charged with collecting from John Tangmoth  15s.
From John Streven 2s.
~~From John Sterre 6d.~~
~~From William Keche 12d.~~
~~From William Crokker 12d.~~
 Etc. paid

[page 15]
From John Sterre for a fine 6d.
From William Keche for a fine 12d.
From William Crokker for a fine 12d.
From Robert Burgh for a fine 6d.
From Thomas Porter for a fine 6d.
From William Wykes for a fine 3d. paid
From Thomas Benet for a fine 6d.
From John Lyllyng for a fine 6d.
From John Lang for a fine 6d.
From [Blank]
Total [Blank]

[page 16, blank]

[page 17]
Let it be remembered that on Sunday after the Feast of the Finding of the Holy Cross AD 1477, Richard Orchard and John Hulle were elected as stewards for an Ale sold in honour of Saint George the Martyr. They rendered for the ale sold 19s. in cash. They rendered in money which they had previously 6s. 8d.
Total sum 25s. 8d.

And they elected new stewards for the next year, namely John Lyllyng and John Hoper junior. And each of them has in hand 12s. 2d.

Total 25s. 8d.

From the Light of St. George
Let it be remembered that on the Sunday before the Feast of the Purification of the
Blessed Virgin Mary 20 Edward IV [1481], Hugh Andrew and John Hoper came and
they presented their account for the Ale of that year and they rendered 15s. 4d.
And they elected new wardens for the next year namely [blank].

[page 18, blank]

[page 19]
Stephen Davy 2d.
John Forsey 2d.
William Helyer 2d.
John Palmer 2d.
Thomas Stockefysch 2d.
Nicholas Hore 2d.
Thomas Stockfysch 2d.  }
John Forsey 2d.                    } for the drinking in the 34th year
Nicholas Hore 2d.         }

[page 20, *The ordinances or rules of the Fraternity*]

It is ordained that brothers and sisters who are absent on the day of the reckoning,
that is on the Tuesday after Easter, should pay ½ lb of wax, unless they have reasonable
cause.
The said candles should be lit at the Great Altar of the Body of our Lord Christ at the
time of the Elevation of the Host on Sundays and other feast days.
Everyone should pay one penny for the soul of the deceased in respect of all deceased
brothers and sisters of the said Fraternity.
And the said candles should burn while the deceased is buried, and the said wardens
will distribute to the priests for the soul of the deceased.
And it is ordained that each torch will weigh 26 lb.

[page 21, *torn – first word(s) missing*]
2s. 5d. in William Bowley's keeping for the salary of the priest of St Nicholas of Bridport

[page 22, *what appear to be just doodles to work in a re-cut quill, a partial reading may be a
repetition of the words from John 1. 6:*]
There was a man sent from God.
[*Below are a number of doodled names*]    Johe, Johanes, Johes Baktom, William [or]
Witham.

**CD22.** [*A small book relating to the Fraternity of St Katherine, covering period 1428 to 1479*].

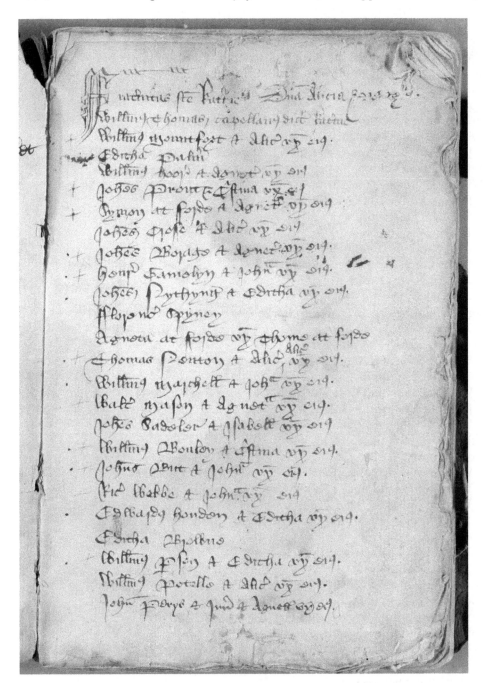

*The first page of DC-BTB/CD/22, names of the members of the Fraternity of St Katherine*

[page 1 blank]
[page 2, *a fragment from Accounts and election of wardens*]
... Gamelyn.
For the soul of Agnes Forde....
Richard Burgh through the pledge of Robert Scarlet and Robert Burgh
Joan Gamelyn through the pledge of J. Crips and W. Helier

[page 3]
Fraternity of St. Katherine       Dame Alicia Beminster
William Thomas chaplain of the said Fraternity
+ William Mountfort and Alice his wife
Edith Palmer
William Hoor and Agnes his wife
+ John Prout and Christine his wife
+ Symon at Forde and Agnes his wife
John Crosse and Alice his wife
+ John Borage and Agnes his wife
+ Henry Gamelyn and Joan his wife
John Nythyng and Edith his wife
Florence Spyney
Agnes at Forde wife of Thomas at Forde
+ Thomas Neuton and Alice his wife
William Marchell and Joan his wife
+ Walter Mason and Agnes his wife
John Sadeler and Isabel his wife
+ William Bouley and Christine his wife
+ John But and Joan his wife
+ Richard Webbe and Joan his wife
Edward Houden and Edith his wife
Edith Browne
+ William Parson and Edith his wife
William Potelle and Alice his wife
John Perys and junior and Agnes his wife

[page 4, *top of page torn*]
... ... es Spy... chaplain there
... Olyver, Joan his wife
Robert Scarlet, Alice his wife
Richard Burgh, Agnes his wife [*added in different ink*] and Alice his wife
Robert Burgh and Margaret his wife
John Crips, Edith his wife
William Howse, Alice his wife
William Helier, Joan his wife
John Algare, Lucy his wife
[*Added in margin*] John Ablee and Eleanor his wife

each of them one pound of wax
John Hille mercer and Joan his wife
[*Added in margin*] John Halle, peyntter [*i.e. painter*]
John Forshey and Emma his wife
John Benet and Christine his wife
Each 6d.
[*Added in margin*] William Sheter and Alice his wife, 6s.
And for one 'folet' of cotton 6d.
Thomas Stocfysch and Agnes his wife
James Berteram and Alice his wife
Increment 7s.
+ Alice Muntigu 6d.
John Atkyn and Margaret his wife
John Williams and Joan his wife
Each of them 6d., that is to say 12d.
Thomas Wey and Joan his wife 6d.
John Maunsell and Agnes his wife 6d.
John Hulle and Agnes his wife 6d.
John Waryner and Joan his wife ½ lb of wax

[page 5]
The accounts of William Bouley and John Borage, wardens of the Fraternity of St. Katherine the Virgin, on St. Thomas's Day in Christmas week, 7 Henry VI [1428]. They rendered £5 13s. 4d. Each of them for himself ~~received~~ rendered 56s. 8d. And they again elected wardens, namely John But and John Nythyng; and, as pledges for the aforesaid John But, John Burges and William Bouley; and, as pledges for John Nythyng, Thomas Neuton and Richard Brangewayne. The aforesaid wardens received into their custody in turn £5 13s. 4d.

The accounts of John But and John Nythyng, wardens of the Fraternity of St. Katherine the Virgin, on the day of St. John the Apostle 8 Henry VI [1429]. They rendered five pounds and thirteen shillings and ~~8d.~~ 4d. And they elected Henry Gamelyn through the pledges of William Bouley and John But; and William Potell through the pledges of John Borage and Richard Brangewayne. And each of these wardens received into his custody 56s. 8d. Total sum: £5 13s. 4d.

[page 6]
The accounts of Henry Gamelyn and William Potell, wardens of the Fraternity of St. Katherine the Virgin, on the day of St. John the Apostle 9 Henry VI [1430]. They rendered £5 13s. 4d. And they elected Thomas Neuton through the pledges of William Mountfort and William Bouley; and William Parson through the pledges of Walter Mason and John Borage. And each of these wardens received into his custody 56s. 8d. Total sum: £5 13s. 4d.

The accounts of Thomas Newton and William Parson, wardens of the Fraternity of

St. Katherine the Virgin, on the day of St. John the Apostle 10 Henry VI [1431].
They rendered £5 13s. 4d. And they elected Thomas Newton through the pledges of
William Bowley and John But; and William Parson through the pledges of John But
and Richard Brangwayne. And each of these wardens received into his custody 56s.
8d.
Total sum: £5 13s. 4d.

Bowley and John Burges and each of these wardens received 50s
Total £5

[page 7]
The accounts of Thomas Newton and William Parson, wardens of the Fraternity of St.
Katherine the Virgin, on the day of St. John the Apostle 11 Henry VI [1432]. They
rendered £5 0s 4d. And they elected new wardens for the next year namely Thomas
Newton through the pledges of William Bowley and John But; and William Parson
through the pledges of John But and Richard Brangwayne. And each of these wardens
received into his custody 56s. 8d.
Total sum: £5 13s. 4d.

Accounts presented on the day of St. John the Apostle for the Fraternity of St.
Katherine the Virgin, 12 Henry VI [1433]. Thomas Newton and William Parson, the
wardens, came and rendered their account. And they elected new wardens for the
next year namely John Borage through the pledges of William Bowley and Richard
Brangewayne; and Henry Gamelyne through the pledges of John But and Thomas
Newton. And each of them received into his custody 53s. 4d.
Total sum: £5 6s. 8d.

Accounts presented on the day of St. John the Apostle for the brothers of the Fraternity
of St. Katherine 13 Henry VI [1434], and they rendered heard their account. John
Borage and Henry Gamelyn came and rendered their account. And they elected new
wardens for the next year namely Henry Gamelyne through the pledges of John But
and William Parson; and Thomas Newton through the pledges of William. [breaks off
here].

[page 8]
Accounts presented on the day of St. John the Apostle for the brothers of the Fraternity
of St. Katherine 14 Henry VI [1435]. Thomas Newton and Henry Gamelyn, wardens
of the Fraternity of St. Katherine, came and rendered their account. And the brothers
elected wardens, namely Thomas Newton through the pledges of William Bowley and
John Burges; and Henry Gamelyne through the pledges of John But and William
Parson. And each of these wardens received 50s
Total £5.

Accounts presented on the day of St. John the Apostle for the brothers of the Fraternity
of St. Katherine 15 Henry VI [1436]. Thomas Newton and Henry Gamelyn, wardens

of the aforesaid Fraternity, came and rendered their account. And the brothers elected wardens for the next year, namely John But through the pledges of Richard Brangwayne and Henry Gamelyn; and John Burges through the pledges of William Parson and William Bowley. And each of these wardens received 33s. 4d.
Total £3 6s. 8d.

[page 9]
Accounts presented on the day of St. John the Apostle for the brothers and sisters of the Fraternity of St. Katherine 31 Henry VI [1452]. John Burges and Joan, widow of Henry Gamelyn, wardens of the aforesaid Fraternity, came and rendered their account, namely £3 6s. 8d. And they elected new wardens, namely Richard Burgh and Joan Gamelyn; and, as pledges for the aforesaid Richard, Robert Scarlet and Robert Burgh; and, for the aforesaid Joan, John Crips and William Helyer. And the aforesaid wardens received into their custody in turn £3 6s. 8d.
Total £3 6s. 8d.

And they were charged with collecting from nine new brothers, admitted on the aforesaid day. Each of them one pound of wax. Total 9 lbs of wax, as is previously shown in the first folio.

[page 10]
Accounts presented on the day of St. John the Apostle for the brothers and sisters of the Fraternity of St. Katherine 32 Henry VI [1453]. Richard Burgh and Joan, widow of Henry Gamelyn, wardens of the aforesaid Fraternity, came and rendered their account in the presence of the aforesaid brothers and sisters, namely £3 13s. 8d. And they elected new wardens for the next year, namely Richard Burgh through the pledges of Robert Scarlet and John Hille; and John Crips through the pledges of John Algar and William Howse. And the aforesaid wardens received in turn £3 13s. 8d.

Accounts presented on the day of St. John the Apostle for the brothers and sisters of the Fraternity of St. Katherine 33 Henry VI [1454]. Richard Burgh and John Cripse, wardens of the aforesaid Fraternity for one whole year, that is the aforesaid year, came and rendered their account in the presence of the aforesaid brothers and sisters, that is to say £3 13s. 8d. From this £3 13s. 8d., the sum of 27s. was accepted and handed over to William Olyver, for the purchase of two antiphoners, that is to say readers (*anptiphonys videlicet lyecchers*) for the use of the church of the Blessed Mary, Bridport. And so 46s. 8d. remains. And they elected the said Richard and John as wardens for the next year and they received the aforesaid sum, that is 46s. 8d. And through the aforesaid pledges. And the aforesaid wardens received from J. Atkyn and John Williames 12d. Extra.
[page 11]
And so the sum in total is 47s. 8d.

Accounts presented on the day of St. John the Apostle for the brothers and sisters of the Fraternity of St. Katherine 34 Henry VI [1455]. Richard Burgh and John Crips, wardens of the aforesaid Fraternity came and rendered their account, that is to say 47s. 8d. And they elected the above-named wardens through the above-named pledges. They received the aforesaid sum, that is each of the wardens ~~26~~ 23s. 10d.

Accounts presented on the day of St. John the Apostle and Evangelist for the brothers and sisters of the aforesaid Fraternity 35 Henry VI [1456]. Richard Burgh and John Crips, wardens of the aforesaid Fraternity, came and rendered their account in the presence of the aforesaid brothers and sisters, that is 47s. 8d. And they elected the above-named wardens through the above-named pledges. They received the aforesaid sum, that is each of these wardens 23s. 10d. Total 47s. 8d.

[page 12]
Accounts carried out on the day of St. John Evangelist and Apostle for the brothers and sisters of the Fraternity of St. Katherine in the 36th year of the reign of King Henry VI. Richard Burgh and John Crips, wardens of the aforesaid Fraternity, came and rendered their account, namely ~~46s.~~ 47s. 8d. And they elected... [*incomplete entry*].

Accounts presented on the day of St. John Evangelist and Apostle for the brothers and sisters of the Fraternity of St. Katherine 37 Henry VI [1457] after the Conquest. Richard Burgh and John Crips, wardens of the aforesaid Fraternity, came and rendered their account, namely ~~48s. 8d.~~ 49s. 5d. 11d. And they elected new wardens for the next year, namely Richard Burgh through the pledges of William Olyver and Robert Scarlet; and John Crypse through the pledges of William Howse and John Algar. And each of them has in their custody 24s. ~~10d~~ 8½d 11½d.

[page 13]
Accounts presented on the day of St. John Evangelist and Apostle for the brothers and sisters of the Fraternity of St. Katherine 38 Henry VI. Richard Burgh and John Cripse, wardens of the aforesaid Fraternity, came and rendered their account, namely 51s. And they elected new wardens for the next year, Richard Burgh through the pledges of William Olyver and Robert Scarlet; and John Cripse through the pledges of William Howse and John Algar. And each of them has in his custody 25s. 6d.

Accounts presented on the day of St. John Evangelist for the brothers and sisters of the Fraternity of St. Katherine 6 Edward IV [1466]. Richard Burgh and John Crips, wardens of the aforesaid Fraternity, came and rendered their account in this manner, namely 51s. And they elected new wardens for the next year, namely Thomas Weye through the pledges of Richard Burgh and Thomas Cherde; and James Bertram through the pledges of William Olyver and Thomas Stokfyssh. And each of them received in cash 25s. 6d. Total 51s.
And afterwards new brothers and sisters came, namely:
Thomas Cherd, 6d.
William Wikes for the writing (*pro scriptura*)

[page 14]

Accounts carried out on the day of St. John Evangelist 7 Edward IV [1467] for the brothers and sisters of the said Fraternity. To this accounting came Thomas Wey and James Berteram, wardens, and they rendered <sup>for the said year</sup> 51 [s.]. And they elected new wardens for the next year, namely Thomas Wey through the pledges of Richard Burgh and Thomas Cherde; and James Berteram through the pledges of William Olyver and Thomas Stockefysh. And each of them received in cash 25s. 6d.
Total 51s.

And they were charged with receiving from

| | | |
|---|---|---|
| Thomas Cherde | 6d. | |
| and from William Wyke *pro non comparand'* | 6d. | |
| and from John Trygylty | 6d. | |
| from Thomas Porter | | 6d. |
| William Sheter | 6d. | |

[page 15]
Accounts presented on the day of St. John Evangelist 8 Edward IV [1468] for the brothers and sisters of the said Fraternity of Saint Katherine. To this accounting came Thomas Wey and James Berteram, wardens, and they rendered for the said year 54s. 6d. And they elected new wardens for the next year, namely Thomas Wey through the pledges of Richard Burgh and Thomas Cherde; and James Berteram through the pledges of William Olyver and Thomas Stockefysh. And each of them received in cash 54s. 27s. Total 53s. 6d.
From which there remains in hand

| | |
|---|---|
| William Wykys | 6d. |
| Th Cherde | 6d. |

Thomas Bayly and Margery his wife

[page 16]
Accounts presented on the day of St. John Evangelist 9 Edward IV [1469] for the brothers and sisters of the said Fraternity. To this accounting came Thomas Wey and James Berteram, wardens of the said Fraternity, and they rendered for the aforesaid year 52s. 6d. And they elected new wardens for the next year, namely Thomas Wey through the pledges of Richard Burgh and Thomas Cherde; and James Berteram through the pledges of William Olyver and Thomas Stockefyssh. And each of them has in hand 26s. 3d.
Total 52s. 6d.
And they were charged to receive from

| | |
|---|---|
| William Wykys | 6d. |
| And from Thomas Cherde | 6d. |

Accounts presented on the day of St. John Evangelist in the year of Our Lord 1470, in the 49th year from the beginning of the reign of King Henry VI and the first year of his resumption of his reign), for the brothers and sisters of the said Fraternity. To this accounting came Thomas Wey and Robert Warde *in the name of James Berteram*, wardens of the said Fraternity, and they rendered for the ~~next~~ aforesaid year 52s. 6d. And they elected new wardens for the next year, namely Robert Warde through the pledges of William Olyver and Thomas Stockefyssh; and ~~Thomas Sheter~~ William Sheter through the pledges of Richard Burgh and Thomas Porter. And each of them has in hand 26s. 3d. Total 52s. 6d.

And they are charged with receiving from

| | |
|---|---|
| Thomas Cherde | 6d. |
| William Wyke | 6d. |
| Robert Warde | 6d. paid |

[page 17]
Accounts carried out on the day of St. John Evangelist 11 Edward IV [1471] for the brothers and sisters of the said Fraternity. To this accounting came William Sheter and Robert Warde, wardens of the said Fraternity, and they rendered for the aforesaid year 53s. And they elected new wardens for the next year, namely John Cripce through the pledges of William Olyver and John Perie; and William Sheter through the pledges of Richard Burgh and John Hylle. And each of them has in hand 26s. 6d. And they are charged with receiving from Thomas Cherde 6d.

~~Accounts carried out on the Sunday after the Feast of the Circumcision of the Lord, in the year of the Lord 1~~

Accounts carried out on the Sunday after the Feast of the Circumcision of the Lord 19 Edward IV [1479], for the brothers and sisters of the said Fraternity. ~~To this accounting came William Sheter for~~

To this accounting came William Sheter and Constans Cripse, wardens of the said Fraternity, and they rendered for the aforesaid year namely 53s. And they elected new wardens for the next year, namely William Sheter through the pledge of ~~William Rawcreme~~ *John Hylle* and Custans Cripse through the pledge of ~~William Rawcreme~~ *William Olyver*. And each of them has in hand 26s. 6d.

[page 18] *~~Be hyt yn mende tht y have the leverd to Wa[l]ter Thredher for ii s~~ (illegible word) ~~Item the leverd to eodem xvi d Item the leverd eodem ii s et xd Item to the eod[em] iii d~~*

[page 19]
The names of the brothers and sisters of the Fraternity of the Light of the Blessed Katherine of Brid[port], written down on the Sunday before the Feast of the Circumcision of the Lord in AD 1466, 6 Edward IV.

Sir John Spyney chaplain there
William Olyver and Joan his wife
Richard Burgh and Alice his wife
Robert Burgh and Joan his wife
John Cryps and Edith his wife
John Hills and Joan his wife
Thomas Stokfisshe and Agnes his wife
Thomas Warner and Joan his wife

Thomas Weye and Joan his wife
John Perys and Agnes his wife
William Hows and Alice his wife
Alice Scarlett     }
Joan Butte         } widows
Joan Helyare       }
Emma Forshey }

[page 20, blank]

[page 21] ~~Account presented by Henry Gamelyn through the pledges of John (illegible) and William Parson, and Thomas Porter through the pledges of William Boulesey and John Burge, and each of them received 50s.~~
In the fourteenth
Account carried out by Henry Gamelyn through the pledges as before, and Thomas Newton through the pledges as above, and each of them received 50s.

**CD23** *Four title deeds relating to property of the Fraternity of St Katherine*

CD23/1 [*A title deed relating to property of the Fraternity of St Katherine, 1356*]

This indentured agreement, made at Bridport on the Monday before Easter in thirtieth year of King Edward III [18 April 1356], bears witness that John of Axemouth and Joan his wife have handed over and conceded to Alexander Pymor and Joan his wife all that dwelling house, with its yard and its appurtenances, which is situated in Bridport in the lane called Kyllingeslane, and which is known as Snawedon. For Alexander and Joan to have and to hold the aforesaid dwelling house, with yard and appurtenances, for the full term of their lives, or of whichever of them lives the longer, holding quietly and peaceably from the said John and his wife Joan and their heirs. Paying annually to the said John and Joan and their heirs, for the whole term of twelve years after the date of this document, 12d. at the four principal terms of the year, in equal portions. And to the lord King 3d. annually for the St Martin's rent. And after the term of twelve years, the aforesaid Alexander and Joan will pay to John and his wife Joan 20d annually at the four principal terms of the year in equal portions, and the St Martin's rent of 3d. annually for the whole term of the lives of the said Alexander and Joan.
And the aforesaid Alexander and Joan his wife will maintain and keep in repair the aforesaid dwelling house with its appurtenances, and will return it in the same good condition as when they received it or better.
And if it should happen that the aforesaid rent should be in arrears at the aforesaid terms, either in part or wholly, having been asked for, <sup>and they are unwilling to pay within a week</sup>; or if they should cause any waste in the said dwelling house; or if they should transfer it to someone else as a freeholding; then it shall be permissible for the said John and Joan and their heirs to enter into the said dwelling house and to reclaim possession of it without the agreement of the aforesaid Alexander and Joan. And the aforesaid John and Joan and their heirs will warrant, quitclaim and defend the aforesaid dwelling

house with its yard and all its appurtenances for the said Alexander and Joan for the whole term of their lives, or of whichever of them lives the longer, as previously stated, against all mortals. In witness whereof the seals of the aforesaid John, Joan, Alexander and Joan are affixed alternately.

With the following witnesses: William Hichecok, John Lomb, bailiffs at the time, Robert Budde, William Tracy, Thomas Cole, Edward Taillour and others. Dated in the year and place aforesaid.

[*On the reverse, a faded and partially illegible list*]:
Wheat [*illegible words*]
Barley [*illegible words*]
Beans [*illegible words*], 10 qtrs 1 bsh, and sown 2 qtrs, 3 bsh.
Oats, 21 qtrs 5 bsh and allowed 17 [qtrs] 4 bsh, and surplus sown 4 qtrs, 2 bsh.
Price per bsh 3d.

CD23/2 [*A title deed relating to property of the Fraternity of St Katherine, 1380*]

Let all men, now and in the future, know that I, John Tanner, have granted, conceded and with this present charter confirmed to John Goldsmyth and John Passager, wardens of the Lights of the Fraternity of St. Katherine of Bridport and their successors at any given time, all that dwelling house or toft with its appurtenances, situated in the lane called Kyllyngeslane, between the dwelling house of John Axemouth called Snawedon and the yard of John de Chidiok. For the aforesaid John Goldsmyth and John Passager, and their successors at any given time, to have and to hold the aforesaid dwelling house or toft with its appurtenances from the aforesaid John Tanner and his heirs for ever, and from the Lord King in chief, for the services which are due and accustomed by right. And I the aforesaid John and my heirs will warrant and defend the aforesaid dwelling house or toft with its appurtenances for the aforesaid John Goldsmith and John Passager and their successors at any given time against all mortals for ever. In witness whereof I have appended my seal to the present documents.

With the following witnesses: John Tracy and John Hayward, bailiffs at the time, Robert Bemyster, Walter Hasard, William Cordaill, William Crokern and others.

Dated at Bridport on Monday after the feast of St. Lucy the Virgin 4 Richard II [17 December 1380].

CD23/3 [*A title deed relating to property of the Fraternity of St Katherine, 1380*]

To all Christ's faithful to whom the present document shall come, greetings in the Lord from John Axemouth and his wife Joan. Know that we have granted and conceded to John Goldsmyth and John Passager, wardens of the Lights of the Fraternity of St. Katherine of Bridport and their successors at any given time, an annual rental of 20d, due from a dwelling house called Snawdon which Alexander Pymor holds from us in Bridport for the term of his life in Kyllyngeslane; Also the reversion of the aforesaid dwelling house, to take effect after the death of the aforesaid Alexander. For the aforesaid John and John and their successors at any given time to have and to hold the aforesaid annual rental of 20d together with the reversion of the aforesaid dwelling house, to take effect after the death of the aforesaid Alexander, from the Lord King in chief for the services which are due and accustomed by right. And we, the aforesaid John de Axemouth and Joan my wife and our heirs will warrant and defend the aforesaid annual rental of 20d together with the reversion of the aforesaid dwelling house, to take effect after the death of the aforesaid Alexander, for the aforesaid John and John and their successors at any given time against all mortals for ever.

In witness whereof I have appended my seal to the present documents.

With the following witnesses: John Tracy and John Hayward, bailiffs at the time, Robert Bemynster, Walter Hasard, William Crokern and others.

Dated at Bridport on Monday after the feast of St. Lucy the Virgin 4 Richard II [17 December 1380].

CD23/4 [*A title deed relating to property of the Fraternity of St Katherine, 1380*]

Jhesu Mercy [written in the indent at the head of the parchment]

Let all men, now and in the future, know that.. John Goldsmith and John Passager, wardens of the Fraternity, Chantry and Lights of St. Katherine of Bridport, have granted, conceded and with this present charter confirmed to John [B]enesfeld and Joan his wife and the legitimately born heirs of their bodies those two dwelling houses or tofts, which lie in Kyllyngeslane between the dwelling house of the said John Benesfeld and the land of Sir John de Chidiok, and which are called Snawdon. We hold them from the grant of John Exemouth and his wife Joan and John le Tanner.

For the aforesaid John and Joan and the heirs born of their bodies to have and to hold those two dwelling houses or tofts, freely, quietly, well and peacefully by hereditary right for ever. Paying annually for them, to us and our successors at any one time, three shillings sterling at the four principal terms of the year, in equal portions for all service apart from royal service. And the aforesaid John and Joan and their legitimately born heirs will maintain and keep in repair the aforesaid dwelling houses or tofts, and will keep them in a suitable condition.

And the aforesaid John and Joan, for themselves and their heirs, acknowledge that if the aforesaid rent of three shillings, in part, in total or in any portion of it, should happen to fall into arrears by two weeks after the end of any term, then the wardens and their successors will be entitled to enter into the said dwelling houses or tofts, to distrain and to keep any goods distrained, until such time as the wardens and their successors have received full satisfaction in respect of the aforesaid rent. And if they are unable to find distrained goods in the said dwelling houses or tofts sufficient for the rental arrears, then the aforesaid John and Joan concede for themselves and their legitimate heirs that the aforesaid wardens and their successors can [*tear to manuscript, presumably the remainder of the clause is* "retake possession of without obstruction."] the aforesaid dwelling houses or tofts. And we, that is the aforesaid John and John, wardens, and our successors will warrant and defend the aforesaid two dwelling houses or tofts, with all their appurtenances, for the aforesaid John Benefeld and Joan his wife and their legitimately born heirs against all mortals for ever. In witness whereof the aforesaid parties have affixed their seals alternately to the present indented charter.

With the following witnesses: John Tracy, John Hayward, bailiffs at the time, Robert Bemyster, Walter Hasard, William Krokorne, Laurence Bure and others. Dated at Bridport on the Tuesday in the Feast of St Gregory the Pope, 4 Richard II [13 March 1380]. And because our seals may be unknown [*incognita*], we have added the seal of Robert Bemyster.

[*On reverse, apparently in the same hand*]
Let it be remembered that John Axemouth and his wife Joan, John le Tanner and his wife Joan, by unanimous agreement have given to John le Goldsmyth and John Passager, wardens of the aforementioned Fraternity of the Lights of St. Katherine, and their successors at any one time, for the maintenance of a Chaplain or Chaplaincy performing the divine service at the altar of St. Katherine, two dwelling houses or tofts situated in Killyngeslane as described above. Such that any and all profits and rental income from the said dwelling houses or tofts should remain to the said chaplains and their successors for ever. Such that these chaplains should remember and make commemoration at the mass for the souls of John le Hatter, and Christine his wife, John le Tanner and Joan his wife, and John de Axemouth and Joan his wife from day to day without end. And if John Benefeld and his wife Joan should die without any legitimately conceived heirs, as written within, then the two within-mentioned dwelling houses shall remain to the aforesaid wardens and their successors for ever. With Judgement Day as witness, 79s. Recorded

[*In a different hand*]  This is a copy of the indentured agreement for the maintenance of the chaplain of St. Katherine, sealed with three seals.

**CD24** [*A title deed relating to property of the Fraternity of St Katherine, 1369*]

To all Christ's faithful to whom the present document shall come, greetings in the Lord from Richard Ferthyng, Chaplain of the perpetual chantry of St. Katherine of Bridport. Know that I have conceded to Robert Bemynster and Alice his wife one half of the income and profits of my dovecot, to be received annually on whatever day it may chance to be available, for the term of the lives of the said Robert and Alice, from myself and my successors without any opposition or any rent payable. For the said Robert and Alice to have and to hold the aforesaid half of the profits of the said dovecot, for the whole of the lives of the said Robert and Alice, from me and my successors in the aforesaid manner. In witness whereof we have affixed our seals alternately to the present indentured agreement. With the following witnesses: Robert Budde, Richard Snaward, bailiffs at the time, William Henton, Thomas Stanton, and others. Dated at Bridport on Monday after the Feast of the Annunciation of the Blessed Mary, 43 Edward III [26 March 1369].

**CD25** [*A title deed relating to property of the Fraternity of St Katherine, 1388*]

This indenture, made at Bridport on the Thursday after the Feast of the Purification of the Blessed Virgin Mary 11 Richard II [5 February 1388], bears witness that Richard

Stratton, known as Ferthyng, chaplain of the perpetual chantry of St. Katherine of Bridport, has handed over, conceded and surrendered to John Benefeld and Joan his wife the reversion of a tenement, with its appurtenances, to take effect after the death of John Tanner and Joan his wife. The tenement is located in the East Street of the town of Bridport, on the north side, between the tenement of the Master <sup>of the Hospital</sup> of Bridgewater on one side, and a certain tenement belonging to Richard Laurens on the other side. For the aforesaid John and Joan to have and to hold the aforesaid reversion, to take effect on the death of the previously named people, for the whole of the lives of the said John and Joan. For this they are to pay annually to the said Richard and his successors two shillings at the Feast of St Michael for all services except royal service. And if it should happen that the aforesaid John and Joan should die, God forbid, then the reversion of the tenement with its appurtenances should remain to Idonia, the daughter of John and Joan, for the whole life of Idonia, paying annually the rent and services previously stated.

And the aforesaid John and Joan, and Idonia when applicable, concede that if the aforesaid rent of two shillings, in part or in total, should happen to fall into arrears by two weeks after the end of any term, then the said Richard and his successors will be entitled to enter into the said reversion of the tenement, to distrain and to keep any goods distrained, until such time as they have received full satisfaction in respect of the aforesaid rent.

And the aforesaid John and Joan, and Idonia when applicable, shall keep in repair and good order the aforesaid tenement with its appurtenances, after the death of the above-named people, and will return it in as good condition or better than when they received it. And the said Richard and his successors will warrant acquit and defend the aforesaid reversion of the tenement, with its appurtenances, to take effect after the death of the aforenamed people, for the said John and Joan and Idonia as described above against all people. In witness whereof they have affixed their seals alternately. With the following witnesses: John Hayward, Walter Hasard, bailiffs at the time, John Tracy, Edward Tyte, William Cordal, William Crowkern, John Hasard and others. Dated on the day and in the place stated above.

**CD26** [*A title deed relating to property of the Fraternity of St Katherine, 1487*]

To all Christ's faithful who see or hear this indentured agreement, eternal greetings in the Lord from William Tayler and Thomas Elasaunder, cofferers of the borough of Bridport. Know that we, the aforesaid William and Thomas, cofferers, with the consent and agreement of the bailiffs and the whole community of the town, have handed over, conceded and to farm let to Sir John Edward, perpetual chaplain of the chantry of Saint Katherine the Virgin and Martyr of Bridport, one tenement with its appurtenances situated in the South Street of the aforesaid borough of Bridport on the west side, between a plot belonging to John Rendall to the south and a plot recently owned by Richard Lyte to the north. For him to have and to hold the aforesaid tenement with its appurtenances for the term of the life of the aforesaid Sir John Edward, chaplain, from the said cofferers and their successors. He is to pay annually to the Lord King three pence at the feast of St Michael, and nothing besides, for all other services and claims.

And the aforesaid Sir John, chaplain, will keep the aforesaid tenement in sufficiently good repair and order, at his own cost and expense, during the aforesaid term. And we, that is the aforesaid William and Thomas, cofferers, and our successors will, by this present document, warrant and defend the aforesaid tenement with its appurtenances for the term of the life of the aforesaid Sir John, against all people.

In witness whereof, the aforesaid parties have affixed their seals to the present indentured agreement. With the following witnesses: William Rakerayne and Richard Trowbrygge, at the time bailiffs of the town of Bridport, William Stykylpathe, Robert Strowbrygge, John Bremell, William Colmer, Hugh Maneryng, <sup>Richard Orchard</sup> and many others. Dated at Bridport on the Feast of All Saints 3 Henry VII [1 November 1487].

**CD27** [*Two parchment title deeds and one contemporary copy deed relating to property of the Fraternity of St Katherine, 1493*]

CD27/1 [*A title deed relating to property of the Fraternity of St Katherine, 1493, CD27/2 is an identical copy*]

To all Christ's faithful to whom the present document comes, greetings. Know that I, John Burgh of Lyme Regis in the county of Dorset, gentleman, have granted, conceded and by this present charter confirmed to Thomas Cherde and Hugh Mannyng, bailiffs of the town of Bridport and their successors at any given time, two burgage plots with their appurtenances, situated in the East Street of the town of Bridport on the north side, between the tenement of William Borage to the west and the tenement of the heirs of Thomas Stockefysh to the east. For the aforesaid bailiffs and their successors to have and to hold the said two burgage plots from the Lord King for the customary rent and services due by right, for ever.

And I, that is to say the aforesaid John Burgh, and my heirs will warrant and defend, by means of the present documents, the aforesaid two burgage plots with their appurtenances for the said bailiffs and their successors against all people. And in addition I ordain and appoint John Parys and John Hasard to be my true attorneys, jointly and severally, to hand over possession and seisin of the aforesaid two tenements with their appurtenances to the aforesaid bailiffs and their successors. In witness whereof I have affixed my seal to this my indentured document. With the following witnesses: William Hodesfyld, knight, John Byconell, knight, Humphrey Fulford, John Bevyn esquire, William Stykylpathe, Richard Orchard, William Baker, William Colmer and many others. Dated at Bridport on 4 February 8 Henry VII [1493].

[*On reverse, in the same hand*]

The condition of this indented deed is such that all profits and rents from the two tenements, previously described both within and on the other part of the documents, should remain for Sir John Edward, chaplain of the chantry of St. Katherine of Bridport, and his successors at any given time, to pray for the souls of Robert Burgh and his wife Marion, Richard Burgh and his wife Agnes, Robert Burgh, Robert Scarlet and his wife Alice, John Burgh and his wife Alice, and for all the faithful departed. And that the said chaplain and his successors should give to the Rector of that church, as an offering, one penny at the Mass on St. Katherine's Day, for naming any of the aforementioned names of the deceased. Moreover I wish that the said chaplain and his successors should have the profit of the aforesaid two tenements for ever.

CD27/3 [*A title deed relating to property of the Fraternity of St Katherine, 1493*]
To all men to whom this present document shall come, John Burgh of Lyme Regis in the County of Dorset, gentleman, sends greetings in the Lord. Know that I, the aforesaid John, have absolved, released and wholly quitclaimed Thomas Cherde and Hugh Mannyng, bailiffs of Bridport, and their successors at any one time, in respect of any right or claim that I ever had or may in any way have in the future in the two burgage plots situated together in the East Street of the town of Bridport on the north side, between the tenement of William Borage to the west and the tenement of the heirs of Thomas Stockefysh to the east, according to the thrust, form and effect of my two indented charters. In witness whereof I have affixed my seal to the present document. Dated at Bridport on 4 February 8 King Henry VII [1493].

**CD31** [*Three unbound sets of accounts relating to the Fraternity of the Blessed Virgin Mary*

CD31/1 [*The top section of an unbound paper sheet of accounts relating to the Fraternity of the Blessed Virgin Mary, 1462. The account is incomplete*].

The accounts of William Howse, steward of the Light of the Blessed Mary the Virgin, from the week after the feast of the Epiphany of the Lord AD 1461 up to the same feast 1462.

Firstly he answers for rental income, £4 9s. 6d.
Next he answers for the pennies received on the night of Epiphany with the ale, 14s.
    From this there remains in the hands of Richard Hore 10s.
    And the aforesaid William rendered his account for 4s, and more.
Next he answers for the rent of one cow for a year, in the keeping of the wife of J. Boleyn, 20d.
Next he answers for the gift of a woman 2d.
Next for a pair of salt pans, nothing this year
Total £4 10s 3d.

And for the amount received for the past year  £7 3s. 8d.
Total in cash £11 18s. 11d.

From this he asks to be allowed for rent arrears this year:
For the house of John Arundell nothing this year, that is to say, 8s.
Next for Richard Merche, 10s
Next for the house of John Gower, 20s
Next for the tenement of Hilbrond Ellewill, 20d.
Next for the lack of two law-day payments of the same tenement, 12d.
Next for the rent due to the King of the same tenement, 3d.
Next for rent due to be paid by Nicholas Brice, 2s.

Next for the capital rent of the same tenement and the tenement of J. Gower, 6d.
Next for the salary of Sir Richard, the chaplain, for three quarters of the year and seven weeks [blank]
Next for bread and wine for the same chaplain for the same period, 15d.

CD31/2 [*An unbound paper sheet of accounts relating to the Fraternity of the Blessed Virgin Mary, 1473*].

The account of John Hulle, steward of the Fraternity of the Blessed Mary of Bridport on the Sunday after the Feast of the Purification of the Blessed Mary 12 Edward IV [8 February 1473].

Rent: firstly he answers for himself for a piece of land called Frerynorchard, 11s.
Next from John Crokern for the rent of the house of Thomas Mankyswylle, 6s. 8d.
Next from John Sampford for the rent of his tenement, 5s.
Next from John Hoper for the rent of his dwelling house, 3s. 4d.
Next for the rent of a stable at the dwelling house of John Sampford, 5d.
Next from Denis Taylor for his dwelling house, 3s. 6d.
Next from John Bremyll for a piece of land next to St. Michael's Lane, 2s.
Next from Alice Keche for a piece of land in the southern part of the town, 3s. 4d.
Next from William Cornysch for the rent of a barn, 3s.
Next from John Bokerell senior for the rent of his tenement, 6s. 8d.
Next, for Thomas Weye for the rent of one tenement, 5s.
Next from William Englysch for the rent of a tenement, [blank].
Next from the aforesaid William for a fine for a piece of land called Culverhay, 3s. 4d.

Other amounts received:
Firstly he answers for sums collected in the vigil of Epiphany, 3s.
Next for the benefit of an ale, 7s.
Next for mass pennies collected from the Fraternity as is shown in a schedule, 5s.
Next for the legacy of Henry Bonvyld for a brass pot sold for 6s.

Allowances:
From this he asks to be allowed for 1 lock and 2 keys for the house of Denis Taylor, 6d.
Next for the rent due to the Lord King for the same house, £3.
Next for the Lord King ~~for the Lord~~ for the house of John Crokhorne, 3d.
Next for wax and the making of a candle, 9d.
Next for paper for schedules and accounts, 1d.
Next for the writing out of the accounts and the rent arrears, 2d.
          Total [blank]

CD31/3 [*Two paper sheets of accounts relating to the Fraternity of the Blessed Virgin Mary, 1475, stitched together foot to head, Exchequer fashion*].

[Sheet 1]

The account of John Hulle, steward of the Fraternity of the Blessed Mary of Bridport carried out on the Sunday after the Feast of the Purification of the Blessed Mary, 14 Edward IV [5 February 1475]. That is to say for two years, the said year having elapsed and passed, from the Feast of the Lord's Nativity in the twelfth year to the same in the thirteenth year [Christmas 1472 to Christmas 1474].

For the first year:

First he answers for rental income, £3 15s. 7d.

Next he answers answers for sums collected in the vigil of the Lord's Epiphany, 5s.

Next he answers for contributions collected from the brothers and sisters the same year, 7s. 10d.

Next for ale sold the same year, 10s

Next he answers for the legacy of Thomas Molyne 8d.

Next he answers for the legacy of William Honybone, one sheep

Next he answers for the legacy of Edward Jesop's wife, two sheep

Total £4 19s. 1d.

Sums allowed:

From this he asks to be allowed for the salary of the priest (*sacerdotis*), 11s.

Next for bread wine and beer, 3d.

Next for the salary of Sir John Stockefysh, 13s.

Next for bread and wine and beer, 2s. 6d.

Next for the repair of John Samford's tenement, 3s. 8d.

Next for five sacks of lime, 2s. 6d.

Next for five sacks of sand, 5d.

Next for the making of the same, 3d.

Next for the rent of Hilbrond Elwyll's tenement for 2 years, 3s. 4d.

Next for a chest, 5s.

Next for the rent due to the King for the tenement of Denis Tayler, 3d.

Next for two cruets, 5d.

Next for paper, 2d.

Total 42s. 9d.

Total remaining 56s. 4d.

Second year:

The account of the same John, steward of the aforesaid Fraternity. Second year, 14 Edward IV [1474-1475].

First he answers for rental income, £3 15s. 7d.

Next for sums collected in the vigil of the Lord's Epiphany, 6s.

Next he answers for contributions collected from the brothers and sisters the same year, 18s. 6d.

[Sheet 2]

Next he answers for the sale of ale in the same year, 10s
Next he answers for the legacy of John Denslow, 20d
Next he answers for the legacy of Hugh Honybone's wife, one salt pan
Next [blank]
Total £5 11s. 9d.

From this he asks to be allowed:
First for the repairs for John Samford, for 6 sacks of lime, 3s.
Next for 2 sacks of sand, 7d.
Next for making the same, 5d.
Next for one thousand stones, 3s. 4d.
Next for carrying the same, 2d.
Next for 100 laths, 8d.
Next for 400 nails, 6d.
Next for the repair and mending of a *lon'* [or *lou'*], 5d.
Next for a thousand pins, 3d.
Next for three *crett'*, 3d.
Next for [English] *a helyar and hys mane and for ther costs*, 5s. 4d.
Next for bread, wine, beer, 12d.
Next for a piece of timber, 2d.
Next he asks to be allowed for the tenement of Denis Tayler, 3s. 4d.
Next for the tenement of John Samford, 15d.
Next for the tenement of John Hulle, 12 s
Next for a piece of land at Atram which William Syle holds, 2s.
Next for paper, 1d.
Next for writing (covering) 4 years, 2s.
Next John Rugge for a pair of salt pans, 2s.
Next John Rendall for one salt pan, 12d.
Total 39s. 9d.
Total remaining £3 12s.
Total sum for these two years £6 8s. 4d.
Total sum for four years in the time of John Hulle £14 7s.

Next William Olyver answers for Thomas Porter £7 from which he pays Sir John Stockefysh £5 5s. for one year. And so there remains in the hands of William Olyver 35s.

Next from this £14 7s. remains in various people's hands, as is shown by a schedule. In the hands of John Hulle £3 16d.

[Sheet 1 reverse]
And the aforesaid brothers and sisters elected new stewards, namely John Hulle and Robert Stroubrigge.
And the aforesaid stewards elected new wardens for the next year, that is to say: Robert Langer through the pledge of John Hylle, John Tengmowthe through the pledge of

William Howchyn, Robert Wever through the pledge of William Crocker, Thomas Orchard through the pledge of John Dunne, Isabel Mayu through the pledge of Richard Burgh, ~~John~~ Richard Knyfe through the pledge of John Hulle, Joan Brownys through the pledge of Richard Orchard, Stephen Gokey through the pledge of William Rakerayne, [*added in a different hand*] John Rendall through the pledge of John Payer, John Ablee through the pledge of John Bremell. And each of them has in hand 8s. Total £4.

CD31/4 [*An unbound paper sheet of accounts relating to the Fraternity of the Blessed Virgin Mary, 1475-1476. The top of this document is badly torn*]

Account of John Hulle ... ...brigge... of the Fraternity of the Blessed Mary of Bridport delivered there on ... the Feast .... in the 15 Edward IV [1475-1476]

Firstly they answer for the rental income, £4 17s. 11d.
Next they answer for money received on the vigil of the Epiphany of the Lord, 7s.
Next they answer for a total collected from the brothers and sisters the same year, 23s. 2d.
Next for ale sold the same year, 12s.
Next they answer for the legacy of the sister of Nicholas Stevyns, 3d.
Next they answer for the fine of John Lyllyng, 16d.
Next they answer for the fine of Nicholas Baker of Byrton, 12d.
Next they answer for the money received at the last accounts, £14 7s.
Next they answer for the money received from the goods of Sir John Wyne, £6 3s. 5½d.
Total sum: ~~£21 8s. 9d.~~ £27 11s. 2½D

Next they ask for sums to be allowed: firstly for arrears in the last accounts, as is shown in a schedule, £3 16d.
Next for rental income allowed the same year, 40s. 10d.
Next they ask to be allowed for expense incurred as is shown in a schedule, £4 5s. 4½d
Next they ask to be allowed, as is shown in a schedule, for the repair of 2 cottages of Sir John Wyne, £13 8s. 6d.
Total amount of sums allowed, £22 16s. 2d.

Let it be remembered that the 2 cottages of Sir John Wyne owe, thus far, to the Fraternity of the Blessed Mary for expenses incurred, as is shown in a schedule, £7 5s. 0½d.
Total sum left with the 3 stewards in cash, £ 3 15s. 0½d.

Let it be remembered that Joan Olyver, the widow of William Olyver, owes, from the money received from the wife of Thomas Porter still to be paid to the Fraternity of the Blessed Mary, 8s. 4d.

Let the following arrears appearing in this account in hand be remembered:

William Sylle owes for 2 years and 3 terms for Atram's land, 22s.
Next, for the tenement of John Bokerell for 3 years, 20s.
Next, John Crokehorne for the tenement of John Hulle, 10s.
Next, John Rendall for the rent of one salt pan (*plumbi*) for 5 years, 5s.
Total 57s.

New stewards were elected for the next year, namely Robert Strowbrigge and John Hulle, and they have in hand £3 15s. 0½d.

And the aforesaid stewards elected new wardens for the next year, namely: Philip Furber through the pledge of Robert Hulle, Robert Lang through the pledge of John Hylle, John Tengmowthe through the pledge of William Howchyn, Robert Wever through the pledge of William Crocker, Thomas Orchard through the pledge of John Dunne, Isabel Mayu through the pledge of William Rakerayne, Richard Knyfe through the pledge of John Hulle, Stephen Gokey through the pledge of William Rakerayne, John Rendall through the pledge of John Payer, John Ablee through the pledge of John Bremell and each of them has in hand 8s. Total £4.

**CD32**  [*A folded paper sheet of members of the Fraternity of the Blessed Virgin Mary paying the Mass Penny, 1467-1468 and new members admitted in the following year*].

For the mass penny paid. 7 Edward IV [1467-1468]

| | |
|---|---|
| Joan Bolyne | 4d. |
| John Hylbronde | 4d. |
| Edward Storke | 4d. |
| William Knollyng | 4d. |
| John Keche | 4d. |
| John Rugge | 4d. |
| Robert Tyly tailor | 4d. |
| Richard Orchard | 4d. |
| Katherine Stykelane | 4d. |
| Hugh atWey | 4d. |
| John Yung | 4d. |
| John Cobbe | 4d. |
| John Dymmet | 4d. |
| Edward Tracy | 4d. |
| John Dunne | 4d. |
| John Deyr | 4d. |
| John Cripce | 4d. |
| John Cunteryman | 4d. |
| Stephen Akerman | 4d. |
| Stephen Grigory | 4d. |
| Sir Hugh Prior | 4d. |
| John Fyce | 4d. |
| Alice Peuterer | 2d. |

| | |
|---|---|
| John Hylle mercer | 4d. |
| John Payer | 4d. |
| Joan Hore | 4d. |
| William Sheter | 4d. |
| John Bremell | 4d. |
| John Latther | 4d. |
| John Bylke | 4d. |
| John Bolyne | 4d. |
| William Rokerys | 4d. |
| John Saunder | 4d. |
| John Able | 4d. |
| William Browne | 4d. |
| John Rendall | 4d. |
| Robert Payer | 4d. |
| Alice Scarlet | 4d. |
| Sir John Crewys | 4d. |
| Thomas Flete | 4d. |
| Thomas Stockefysh | 4d. |
| John Prior | 4d. |
| John Long | 4d. |
| Thomas Bayly | 4d. |
| Richard Tyly | 4d. |
| John Browne | 4d. |
| Thomas Waryner | 4d. |
| John Mayu | 4d. |
| William Cornysh | 4d. |
| Robert Long | 4d. |
| William Walyse | 4d. |
| Thomas Smert | 4d. |
| Robert Trowbryge | 4d. |
| William Olyver | 4d. |
| Richard Burgh | 4d. |
| John Sterre | 4d. |
| Robert Burgh | 4d. |
| John Trygylty | 4d. |
| Total | 19s. 3d. |
| William Edmunde | 4d. |

(Page 2)

Here is the list of names, newly undertaken, of the brothers and sisters of [the Fraternity of] the Blessed Virgin Mary, living in Bridport, that is to say on the Sunday day before the Feast of the Purification of the Blessed Mary in the 8 Edward IV [29 January 1469], taken from the old names and similarly the new names, according to the information of J. Doget the steward.

Hugh Priour
William Olyver and his wife Joan
John Sterre and his wife Joan
Richard Burgh and his wife Joan
John Harrys and his wife Agnes
Thomas Stokfisch
Robert Burgh and his wife Joan
Thomas Portour and his wife Alice
John Doget and his wife Florence

**CD33** [*A folder paper sheet containing the receipts of the Fraternity of Our Lady, written in English*]

The receyts of the brotherathern of oure Ladye
~~Ferst receyved at xii the nyght vjs. viiid.~~
Item receyved of the be queste of Thom[a]s Sadeller iiijs.
Item of the be queste of John Dyer xijd.
Item for the be queste of Robard Bracy and his doughter viijd.
Item for the be queste of Robard Hasard'is man iiijd.
Item for the be queste of Will[iam] Milleward xijd.
Item for the be queste of the wiff of John Kenyll iijs. & a rynge
Item receyved of Richard Batyn ys fine viijd.
Item of the bequeste of Jone Lokyer        xvjd.
Item of the bequeste of Will[iam] Orchard xxd.
Item of the bequeste of the servaunt of Will[iam] Rawkreme xld.
Item of the bequeste of the servaunt of William Burgeis vjd.
Item of the bequeste of ~~Will~~ Philip Wever viijd.
Item of the bequeste of Raynald Tokere a brasyn crokke of the weight of xxjli
Item of the be queste of Thomas Holard a eu and a wethere
Item of the be queste of John Symmys a eu and a ~~whether~~ lame
Item for the fyne of Harry Jakman a chilver lame
Item of the be queste of Rogger Jolet [or Jelet] ij ewen and ij wethers
Item of the bequeste of Steven Skenner ij wethers and ij euen
Item of the be queste of the son of Thomas Honyborn ij wethers
Item of the be queste of the son of John Bawdyn i shepe
Item of the be queste of Thomas Clerke and his wife iiijs.
Item of the be queste of ~~Goly~~ the doughter of Goly iij shepe
~~Item of the ale y sold xxxs~~
Item of the fine of Richard Whitehorn vjd.
Item for the fine of Will[iam] Pratte, viijd.
Item for the ship y sold to the same Will[iam] vjs. iiijd. the whiche remayneth in his hand
Summa [Total] xxxs. xd.

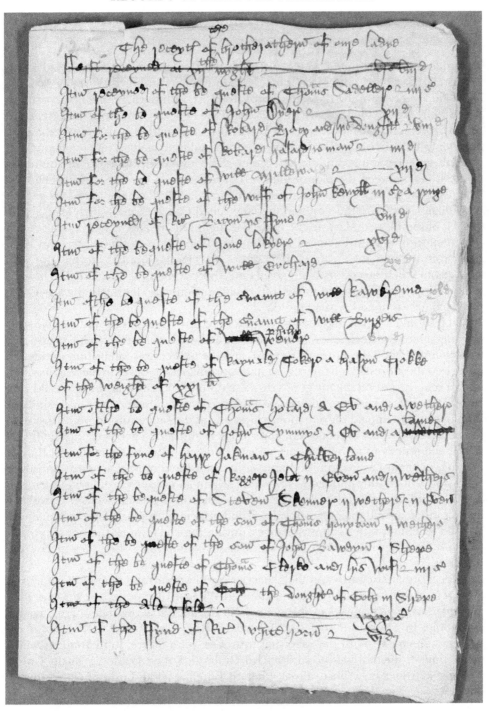

*DC-BTB/CD/33: Receipts of the Fraternity of Our Lady*

**CD34** [*A parchment title deed relating to property of the Fraternity of the Blessed Virgin Mary, 1475*].

This indentured agreement, made at Bridport at the Feast of the Lord's Nativity 15 Edward IV [1475], witnesses that John Hulle and Robert Strawbrygge, stewards of the aforesaid Fraternity of the Blessed Mary of Bridport, with the agreement and consent of the feoffees of all the lands and tenements of the Fraternity, and with the agreement of the brothers and sisters of the said Fraternity, have handed over, conceded and to farm let to William Cornysche and his wife Joan and their assigns, one tenement with its appurtenances situated in the East Street of the town of Bridport on the south side of the street, between the plot of the Lord of Stourton to the north, which Thomas Lyamisse now holds, a close of land belonging to Roger Butte to the south, the garden of William Gendon to the west and the lane called Church Lane, which leads to the church of the Blessed Mary, to the east. For them to have and to hold the aforesaid tenement with its appurtenances until the completion of the term of sixty years from now, from the said stewards and their successors. Paying annually, to the aforesaid stewards and their successors at any given time, three lawful shillings of English money, at the four principal terms of the year in equal portions; also paying to the Lord King the customary rent and services owed.

And if it should happen that the aforesaid rent of three shillings should be in arrears and unpaid for two weeks after any of the terms on which it should be paid, provided it was requested, then the aforesaid stewards and their successors will be fully entitled to enter into the aforesaid tenement with its appurtenances in order to make a distraint, and to remove and retain any goods distrained, until such time as the aforesaid rent with all the arrears has been fully recovered. And if the aforesaid rent of three shillings is in arrears and unpaid for one month after any of the said terms on which it should be paid, provided it was requested, and sufficient distrained goods cannot be found in the said tenement with its appurtenances to meet the aforesaid rent, or if they or any one of them have committed any waste, then the aforesaid stewards and their successors will be fully entitled to re-enter, reclaim and repossess the said tenement, notwithstanding anything in this agreement. And the aforesaid William Cornysche and his wife Joan and their assigns will well and sufficiently repair, mend and maintain the said tenement with its appurtenances, during the said term, at their own expense and cost, and they will hand it back in the same condition as when they received it, or better.

And the aforesaid stewards and their successors will warrant and defend the aforesaid tenement with its appurtenances for the said William Cornysche and his wife Joan and their assigns, by means of this document, during the above-stated term, against all people. In witness whereof the aforesaid parties have affixed their seals to the present agreement. With the following witnesses: John Sterre, John Dunne, bailiffs at the time of the aforesaid town, Richard Orchard, Robert Cowley, William Taylor, Nicholas Cardmaker, William Elyce, Richard Bittellisgate and others. Dated on the day and place stated above.

**CD35** [*A parchment title deed relating to the Fraternity of the Blessed Virgin Mary, 1475*].

This indentured agreement, made at Bridport at the Feast of St Michael the Archangel in the 15 Edward IV [1575], witnesses that John Hulle and Robert Strowbrygge, stewards of the aforesaid Fraternity of the Blessed Mary of Bridport, with the agreement and consent of the feoffees of all the tenements and lands of the Fraternity, and with the agreement of the brothers and sisters of the said Fraternity, have handed over, conceded and to farm let to John Bremell and his wife Alice, and to William and Elizabeth their son and daughter, a piece of land located in St Michael's Lane of Munden's between the land of St. Michael of Munden's to the south, currently held by Thomas Charde, and the land belonging to William Bowley, which John Dunne currently holds, to the north, and a plot which Thomas Tracy now holds to the north (sic). For them to have and to hold the said piece of land with its appurtenances for the term of the life of the said John Bremell and his wife Alice, and their son and daughter William and Elizabeth, or whichever of them lives the longest, from the said stewards and their successors. Paying annually, to the aforesaid stewards and their successors at any given time, two lawful shillings of English money, at the four principal terms of the year in equal portions; also paying to the Lord King the customary rent and services owed.

And if it should happen that the aforesaid rent of two shillings should be in arrears and unpaid for two weeks after any of the terms on which it should be paid, provided it was requested, then the aforesaid stewards and their successors will be fully entitled to enter into the aforesaid piece of land with its appurtenances in order to make a distraint, and to remove and retain any goods distrained, until such time as the aforesaid rent with all the arrears has been fully recovered. And if sufficient distrained goods cannot be found in the said pece of land with its appurtenances to meet the aforesaid rent, or if they or any one of them have committed any waste, then the aforesaid stewards and their successors at any one time will be fully entitled to re-enter, reclaim and repossess the said tenement, notwithstanding anything in this agreement. And the aforesaid John Bremell and his wife Alice, and their son and daughter William and Elizabeth will well and sufficiently repair, mend and maintain the said piece of land with its appurtenances, during the term of the life of the said John and Alice his wife, and their son and daughter William and Elizabeth, or whichever of them lives the longest, at their own expense and cost.

And the aforesaid stewards and their successors will warrant and defend the aforesaid piece of land with its appurtenances for the said John Bremell and his wife Alice, and their son and daughter William and Elizabeth, by means of this document, during their lives or that of one of them living the longest, against all people. In witness whereof the aforesaid parties have affixed their seals to the present agreement. With the following witnesses: Richard Burgh, John Dunne, bailiffs at the time of the aforesaid town, Richard Orchard, Thomas Bayly, John Tregaltys, William Rawkerayne, Richard Byttelisgate and others. Dated on the day and place stated above.

**CD36** [*A parchment title deed relating to the Fraternity of the Blessed Virgin Mary, 1530*].

To all Christ's faithful to whom the present indented document comes, eternal greetings in the Lord from John Isaac and William Trenchard, wardens of the Fraternity of the Blessed Mary, of the town of Bridport. Know that we, the said John and William, have, with the assent and consent of the bailiffs and of the whole Council of the Town, handed over, conceded and to farm let to Henry Harman and his assigns one tenement with its appurtenances situated in the South Street of the aforesaid town, on the east side of that street, between the land of John Cottell to the south and the burgage plot of Thomas Molleyns to the north, abutting the land of the said John Cottell to the east. For Henry Harman and his assigns to have and to hold the aforesaid tenement with its appurtenances from the day of the making of the present document to the end and completion of a term of 80 years following from then.

Paying annually to the aforesaid wardens and their successors at any one time ten shillings of legal English money at the four principal terms of the year, and paying to the Lord King the rent and services due to him.

And if it should happen that the aforesaid rent of two shillings should be in arrears and unpaid, in part or in whole, for two weeks after any of the terms on which it should be paid (provided it was requested in the due manner), and if sufficient distrained goods cannot be found in the said tenement with its appurtenances to meet the aforesaid rent, or if they commit any waste, then the aforesaid stewards and their successors at any one time will be fully entitled to re-enter, reclaim and repossess the said tenement, notwithstanding anything in this agreement.

And the said wardens and their successors will well and sufficiently repair, mend and maintain the said tenement, during the aforesaid term, at their own expense and cost. And the aforesaid wardens and their successors will warrant and defend the aforesaid piece of land with its appurtenances for the said Henry and his assigns, by means of this document, during the aforesaid term, against all people.

In witness whereof the present parties have affixed their seals alternately to the present agreement. With the following witnesses: Robert Hasard junior, William Charde junior, bailiffs at the time of the said town, William Charde senior, Thomas Brownyng, Richard Davage and others. Dated at the aforesaid Bridport on the fourth day of January 21 Henry VIII [1530].

**CD37** [*A parchment title deed relating to the Fraternity of the Blessed Virgin Mary, 1475*].

To all Christ's faithful to whom this present indented document shall come, Thomas Norys and William Moxsage, wardens of the Fraternity of the Blessed Mary of Bridport, send greetings in the eternal Lord. Know that we, the aforesaid Thomas and William, with the agreement and the consent of the bailiffs and burgesses of the whole community of the town, have handed over, conceded and let to Stephen Kyrsey and his assigns one barn which lies in a lane called Irysche Lane, in the western part of that street between the land of John Butte to the south and the land of Robert Hasard to the north; and also half an acre of arable land lying in the southern part of the same town, next to the mill of John Salmon. To have and to hold the aforesaid barn and half acre of land with their appurtenances to the said Stephen and his assigns from the day of the making of this present document to the end of a term of sixty years following from that time and fully to be completed. Paying from them every year to the aforesaid wardens and their successors whoever they might be at the time three shillings of legal English money at the four principal terms of the year, that is to say paying at the feasts of Christmas, the Annunciation of the Blessed Virgin Mary, the Nativity of Saint John the Baptist and the feast of Saint Michael the Archangel, in equal portions; and performing all other duties and services which are due from these properties and customary. And if it should happen that the aforesaid rent of three shillings should be in arrears and unpaid, in part or in whole, for fifteen days after any of the aforesaid feasts on which, as stated, it should be paid (provided it was requested), and if sufficient distrained goods cannot be found in the said barn and other premises with their appurtenances, then we the aforesaid wardens and our successors will be fully entitled to re-enter, reclaim and repossess the said barn and other premises, notwithstanding anything in this lease. And we, truly, the aforesaid wardens and our successors will warrant and defend the aforesaid barn and other premises with their appurtenances for the said Stephen and his assigns, by means of this document, during the aforesaid term, against all people. In witness whereof the present parties have affixed their seals alternately to the present agreement. With the following witnesses: John Orcharde and Nicholas Lamisham, bailiffs of the said town at the time; Robert Hasard junior, Richard Davage, William Trenchard and many others. Dated at Bridport on the twelfth day of October 20 Henry VIII [1528].

**CD50** [*A folded sheet of accounts relating to the Fraternity of the Holy Cross in the Chapel of St Andrew's Bridport, dated 1470*]

[page 1] Accounts for the Sunday after the Feast of the Lord's Epiphany 1470, being the 49th year from the beginning of the reign of King Henry VI and the first year after his restoration to the kingdom. The wardens of the said Fraternity, namely John Trygylty and John Dunne came and rendered their account. And they elected [the paragraph ends here].

Accounts for the Sunday after the Feast of the Lord's Epiphany 12 Edward IV [10 January 1473]. John Trygylty and John Dunne came and rendered their account. And they elected new wardens for the next year, namely John Trigylty through the pledge of William Olyver and John Perys and John Dunne through the pledge of John Hylle and Thomas Stockefyssh. And each of them has in hand John Trigylty has in hand 23s. and John Dunne has in hand 19s. Also there remains in the hands of John Tengmowthe 20s 7d., as can be seen by the previous account. From this the said John Tengmowthe has promised to pay 20d each term.
Next they were charged with collecting from Richard Burgh 6d.

[page 2] Accounts for the Sunday after the Feast of the Lord's Epiphany 13 Edward IV [9 January 1474]. John Trygylty and John Dunne, stewards of the Fraternity of the Holy Cross in the Chapel of Saint Andrew, came and rendered their account. And

they elected new wardens for the next year, namely John Trigylty through the pledge of William Olyver and John Perys and John Dunne through the pledge of Thomas Stockefyssh and John Hylle.

And John Trigylty received the sum which he had the previous year [that is 23s.] And John Dunne has the same sum which he had the previous year [that is 19s.] And John Tengmowthe came to this account and paid 3s. 4d. from a total of 20s 8d. [7d.] and promised to pay 3s. 4d. at the Easter following the date of this present document, and 20d each subsequent term of this year to the aforesaid wardens. And so he must pay for 2 years 13s. 4d. And John Trigylty received 23s. and John Dunne received 23s. 5d.

**CD51** [*Two parchment deeds relating to property of the Fraternity of the Holy Trinity*]

CD51/1 [*Deed relating to property of the Fraternity of the Holy Trinity, 1271*]

In the year of grace 1271 at the feast of the Lord's Resurrection this agreement was made between William son of Richard Killing of Bridport of the one part and Eudo the merchant and cofferer of the Fraternity of Holy Trinity constituted in the same town of the other part; that is to say that the said William, as he is fully entitled to do, has handed over, conceded and let, on behalf of himself and his heirs or assigns, one dwelling house belonging to him in the town of Bridport. He obtained this dwelling house with its curtilage from the grant and concession of Elias of Porstok. It is situated in the East Street of the same town, near the land of Richard Muchey to the west. To have and to hold the said dwelling house with its curtilage from the aforesaid William and his heirs and assigns to Eudo and the aforesaid Confraternity of the Trinity and their assigns, freely, quietly, peacefully and completely, without the diminution of any part, to the full completion of the term of eight years next following, for 19 shillings of sterling, which the aforesaid Eudo, in the name of the said members of the Fraternity, has paid into the hands of the said William for all secular service and all manner of charge or demand. And if the aforesaid members of the Fraternity carry out any repairs to the building of the aforesaid dwelling house, through the failure of William and his heirs or assigns to carry them out, then the length of the term of this letting shall be increased proportionately to the increase in expenses incurred in repairing the house. Moreover if the said William and his heirs or assigns do not pay 4 shillings annual rent to the said members of the Fraternity or their assigns (as is set out and declared in a letter of obligation drawn up), then all that stall with its appurtenances which is joined to the dwelling house shall remain in the possession of the members of the Fraternity or their assigns by as many years' increase in the lease as there are shillings unpaid. The aforesaid William and his heirs or assigns shall warrant and defend all the matters detailed above to the aforesaid members of the Fraternity or their assigns against all mortals, and will acquit them of any damage or loss incurred in the aforesaid letting.

Richard Killing, father of the aforesaid William, has undertaken to make good all defects in the rents, at the wish of the said members of the Fraternity and their assigns, without any contradiction or obstruction whatsoever in the world. Moreover the aforesaid William and his heirs, during the aforesaid term, shall not give, sell, hand over as security for a loan, or assign in any other way the said dwelling house with its stall to anybody in the world, including the members of the Fraternity, other than to Richard Killing his father.

Both the said Richard and the said William have pledged faithfully to observe all these matters by joining hands with the said Eudo. And so that this agreement might be more secure the said Richard and William for the one part and the said Eudo for the other part have affixed their seals alternately to the present document in the form of a deed. With the following witnesses: John Skyberd; Stephen Rose; William Skyberd; Richard de Ramesham; Walter Stocfot; John Notting; Walter Hux and others.

CD51/2 [*Deed relating to property of the Fraternity of the Holy Trinity, undated, circa 1280*]

Let all men, now and in the future, know that I, Elias de Porstok, have granted, conceded and by this present deed confirmed on behalf of myself and my heirs to William, son of Richard Killing of Bridport all that house with its curtilage which is situated in the East Street of Bridport between the land of the same William (which he obtained from the grant of Richard Killing) and the land of Richard Hore.

To have and to hold all the aforesaid house with its curtilage to the said William and his heirs or assigns, in chief from the Lord King, through the service and customs due to it, freely, quietly, well and in peace by hereditary right for ever. And for this grant, concession and the confirmation of this deed the said William has given me twenty six silver shillings in hand.

I, Elias, and my heirs will warrant and defend all the aforesaid house with its curtilage to the said William and his heirs or assigns against all men and women for ever.

And in order that my grant concession and the confirmation of this my present deed should continue to be approved and valid for all time, I have validated the present deed with the impression of my seal. With these witnesses: Richard Chynne; Stephen Aylmund; Stephen Rose; Hugh de Roþiny; John de Waudiz and many others.

**CD52** [*A parchment deed relating to property of the Fraternity of the Holy Trinity, undated, circa 1280*]

To all Christ's faithful to whom the present document shall come, eternal greetings in the Lord from Eudo, merchant of Bridport. Know that I, with the assent and goodwill of the brothers and sisters of the Fraternity of the Holy Trinity in the town of Bridport have granted and conceded and confirmed with this present deed to Henry of Krideton, merchant, all that tenement with its appurtenances which I bought from William Killing in the same town and all that land with its appurtenances which is in the South Street of the same town beyond the bars, which I bought from Matilda the widow of Adam Stoldeford. To have and to hold all the aforesaid tenement and all the aforesaid land with all their appurtenances from the said brothers and sisters and their successors, to the said Henry and whoever might be his wife and their heirs or assigns, freely, quietly, peacefully and wholly for ever. Paying annually, from the tenement that used to belong to William Killing, twelve pence to the Mass of the Blessed Mary at the four principal terms of the year.

And from the houses beyond the bars, two pounds of wax or twelve pence to the Abbey of Abbotsbury at the Feast of the Blessed Michael. Also one pound of wax or six pence to the Abbey of Forde, at the will of the tenant. And from the aforesaid tenements and land, six shillings to the Holy Trinity at the annual remembrance of the deceased brothers and sisters of the said Fraternity. Also that they should ensure that a mass is celebrated annually on any week in the name of the Holy Trinity both for the living and for the deceased of the said Fraternity and for all their benefactors. And if any amount of the aforesaid shillings should not be put to the aforesaid uses for the holding of masses, it should revert to the increase of the funds of the said Fraternity. And the said Henry and whoever might be his wife and their heirs and assigns shall undertake all obligations associated with the said tenement and land, whether royal or otherwise, at their own expense.

And if it should happen that my wife Emma should die before me, and the said Henry and his wife or heirs are not able fully to guarantee the payment of the monthly memorial service, it will be permissible for me to enter into the tenement which used to belong to William Killing and to stay there, free from all demands of rent or other charge, for the whole of my life, in possession of all easements without any condition whatsoever.

And we the aforesaid brothers and sisters and our successors will warrant and defend all the above to the said Henry and whoever might be his wife and their heirs and assigns against all people as said above through the said rents. And so that all this should remain approved and valid for all time, I, the aforesaid Eudo, have arranged for the seal of the community of our Fraternity, along with my own seal, to be affixed to the part of this deed which will remain in the possession of the said Henry and his family; and the said Henry, on behalf of himself and his family, with plighted faith and having touching the sacred relics, has affixed his seal to the part that will remain in the keeping of the said Fraternity. With these witnesses: Peter de Ramesham, Nicholas Prikepeny, bailiffs of the same town at the time; Richard de Ramesham; Clement de Eysse; Edward his brother; Roger de Stapelford; Walter Stocfot; John Tapin; Roger de Halcumb; John de Krideton; John de Ramesham; Thomas le Drake, Robert Wyp and others.

**CD53** [*A parchment deed relating to property of the Fraternity of the Holy Trinity, undated, circa 1280*]

Let all men both now and in the future know that I Matilda, lately wife of Adam de Staldeford, in my free and lawful widowhood, in pure and perpetual charity for the soul of the said Adam and for my own soul, have granted, conceded released and quitclaimed for ever to the recently constituted Fraternity of the Holy Trinity in the chapel of Saint Andrew any right that I have had in the past or can have in the future in two dwelling houses with their appurtenances which adjoin each other in the South Street of Bridport, between the land of Stephen Aylmund and the land which at one time belonged to Robert Hole, outside the bars on the eastern side of that street.

The aforesaid Adam, my late husband, as he was fully entitled to do, bequeathed these dwelling houses to God and to the said Fraternity, to support a chaplain in the aforesaid chapel for all time, to celebrate masses for all Christ's faithful alive and dead. To have and to hold the said dwelling houses with their appurtenances to God and to the said Fraternity, holding in chief from the King, freely and quietly without diminution of any part for ever, through the service that is owed and customary. Paying to the Abbey of Abbotsbury twelve pence at the time of the feast of Saint Michael. Also to the Abbey of Forde six pence or one pound of wax, at the said feast, and this at the will of the tenant, for all manner of secular services, actions and demands. In testimony whereof I have affixed my seal to the present deed. With these witnesses: Stephen Aylmund; John Skyberd; Richard de Axeminster; Stephen Rose; Richard de Ramesham; Clement de Eysse; Robert Wyppe and others.

**CD54** [*A parchment deed relating to property of the Fraternity of the Holy Trinity, undated, circa 1280*]

To all Christ's faithful to whom the present document shall come, eternal greetings in the Lord from Thomas le Sule of Bridport. Know that I have granted and conceded and confirmed with this present charter, on behalf of myself and my heirs, to God and to the Fraternity of the Holy Trinity in the chapel of the Blessed Andrew in Bridport, in pure and perpetual charity, for the souls of my father and mother and of my wife Alice, and for the souls of all the faithful departed, one dwelling house with its curtilage which is located in the southern side of the western bridge of this town, between my gate and the course of the river, extending in length from the said bridge to the little tower standing by the water. To have and to hold the said dwelling house with its curtilage and all its appurtenances, to God and the said Fraternity, from me and my heirs or assigns, quietly, peacefully and wholly for ever. Paying from it annually to me, my heirs or assigns one rose at the Nativity of St John the Baptist in the church of Saint Andrew of the same town. I, Thomas, and my assigns will warrant defend and aquit the said dwelling house with its curtilage and all its appurtenances to God and the said Fraternity against all mortals as long as the said rent is paid for ever.
In testimony whereof I have affixed the impression of my seal to the present deed. With these witnesses: John Skibard; Stephen Aylmund; Stephen Rose; Henry Ganet; Richard de Axemenister; Clement de Esse; Peter de Ramesham and others.

**CD55** [*A parchment deed relating to property of the Fraternity of the Holy Trinity, undated, circa 1280*]

Let all men now and in the future know that I, Mabel, widow of Terric Maulard of Bridport, in my pure and lawful widowhood, have granted and conceded and confirmed with this present charter for ever, for the soul of the aforesaid Terric and for my soul and for all the souls of the faithful departed, to God and to the Fraternity of the Holy Trinity in the chapel of the Blessed Andrew in Bridport, four pence of annual rent from the land which we held by the grant and concession of Roysse, the daughter of the late William Bevyn of Bristol, in the town of Bridport. Paying annually to the wardens of the goods of the said Fraternity at the feast of St Michael for ever without further delay. And I, Mabel, and my heirs or assigns will warrant the said four pence of annual rent to the said Fraternity against all people, and will pay it at the said term for ever.

In testimony whereof I have affixed my seal to the present document. With these witnesses: John Skyberd; Peter de Ramesham, bailiffs of the town of Bridport at the time; Clement de Eysse; Eudo the merchant; Richard de Ramesham; Nicholas Benegir; Robert Quarel; Roger Koc junior; Robert Wyppe and others.

**CD56** [*A small book relating to the Fraternity of St Mary and St James, covering period 1406 to 1454*]

[Inside front cover]
What Walter Siffirwast, in 1408 ...

[page 1]
Here are the names of the brothers and sisters of the Fraternity of St. Mary the Virgin and St. James the Apostle which is based at the chapel of St Andrew the Apostle in Bridport, and which was begun at the feast of St. John the Baptist in 1406, namely:
Sir John Cabyn
Sir Robert Axmoth
William Hore and his wife Edith
Adam Hasard and his wife Joan, [*added in a different ink*] and his wife Margaret
William Butt and his wife Emota
Nicholas Barbour and his wife Joan, William their son
Adam Bouley and his wife Christine
William Bal and his wife
Robert Clerke and his wife
Richard Douke and his wife Clarice
John Symones glover and his wife
William Mourton and his wife
John Notyngham and his wife Joan
John Douke and his wife
John Walle and his wife Katherine
Robert Gollop and his wife Clare
William Gollop
John Boudich and his wife Isabel
Stephen Webbe and his wife [*added in a different ink*] Elena
William Skynner and his wife [*added in a different ink*] Alice
Thomas Mankeswell and his wife Julia [*added in a different ink*] Joan

[page 2]
William Touker and his wife Elisota
Thomas Clerk
Henry Clerk
Gregory Davy and his wife Joan
Walter Saundres [*added in a different ink*] and his wife Cristina

John Mankeswell and his wife ~~Margery~~ [in two different inks] Joan Emmota
John Ovyat [*added in a different ink*] and his wife Florence
Walter Clerk [*added in a different ink*] and his wife Isota
John Gouky junior and his wife
Roger Davynter and his wife Joan, Margery his mother
Walter Syffrawast and his wife
William Marchall [*added in a different ink*] and his wife Joan
Richard Dewy and his wife Alice
William Couk and his wife Alice
Thomas Couk carpenter and his wife
William Hethman and his wife
William Stour and his wife Joan
[*Names from this point added in what appears to be the ink used for the annotations above*].
William Pawe
John Pawe and his wife Margaret
John Brode and his wife Alice
William House and his wife Alice
William Olyver and his wife Joan
John Sterre and his wife Lucy
John Dyer and his wife Christine
Walter Warde and his wife Joan
John Boleyn junior and his wife Alice
~~Stephen~~ Gregory Webbe and his wife Joan

[page 3, *Rules or ordinances of the Fraternity*]
Let it be noted that it was so ordained among the aforesaid brothers and sisters, by unanimous consent, that each of the members of the Fraternity shall pay annually, towards the maintenance of the lights and candles in the aforesaid chapel, one penny. Next it is ordained that all brothers and sisters should be present together at the first office of the dead and mass on the day of the burial of any deceased brother or sister. Next it is ordained that all candles should burn continually while mass is sung for any deceased brother or sister. Next it is ordained and conceded that if any brother or sister of the aforesaid Fraternity falls into such a state of poverty that he or she does not have, from their own resources, enough to sustain or help themselves, then they should receive every week from every brother one farthing, until he or she recovers. Next it is ordained that every brother should pay one mass penny to the wardens, in order that they should distribute the pennies to the priests, to pray for the soul of the deceased brother or sister. Next it is ordained that new wardens should be elected with the agreement of the wardens of the previous year, and two more with the agreement of all brothers, and if anyone refuses this agreed procedure they should pay one pound of wax. Next it is ordained that if anyone from the said Fraternity, within a distance of one mile from the parish of Bridport, takes their departure from the life of this world, or is killed by some misfortune, or is drowned through the perils of the sea, and if his or her body is found, then the body should be carried by the aforesaid brothers to a burial place where it can most

conveniently be buried, at the expense of the deceased, if he or she has sufficient wealth, or if not at the expense of the said Fraternity. And if anyone is unwilling to keep to these agreements, or if they refuse to attend the above-mentioned occasions, unless prevented by a reasonable cause, then they will pay to the store of the aforesaid Fraternity one pound of wax.

[page 4]
And in order that each and every one of the aforesaid agreements and ordinances should be kept and observed in the said manner and fulfilled in every detail, the aforesaid brothers and sisters, by unanimous agreement, have faithfully taken their corporal oaths by touching in turn God's sacred Gospels. In witness whereof they caused all this to be written down in the aforesaid year of the reign of King Henry.

[*Annotation, in a different hand*] Next it is ordained that new wardens should maintain candles and so they should pay for the making of the said candles and they received nothing for this.

Let it be noted that on the Sunday after the feast of St. Botolph in the year AD 1407, William Morton and Richard Dewy, wardens of the said Fraternity, rendered their account in the presence of the above-named brothers and sisters and they elected new wardens, namely Walter Syferwast through the pledge of Nicholas Barbour and William Skynner through the pledge of Robert Gollop. And they have in their keeping 14s. 1d.

Let it be noted that on the Sunday after the feast of St. Botolph in the year AD 1408, Walter Syffirwast and William Skynner, wardens of the said Fraternity, rendered their account in the presence of the above-named brothers and sisters and they elected new wardens, namely William Morton through the pledge of Roger Davyngtre and William Bal through the pledge of Nicholas Barbour. And they have in their keeping 18s. 8d.

Let it be noted that on the Sunday after the feast of St. Thomas the Martyr in the year AD 1409, William Morton and William Bal, wardens of the said Fraternity, rendered their account in the presence of the above-named brothers and sisters and they elected new wardens, namely John Glover through the pledge of John Goky and William Touker through the pledge of Nicholas Barbour. And they have in their keeping 18s. 8d. And these new wardens must collect from the brothers and sisters 8d. which is unpaid from rent.

[page 5]
Let it be noted that on the Sunday after the feast of St. Thomas the Martyr in the year AD 1410, John Glover and William Tuker, wardens of the said Fraternity, rendered their account in the presence of the above-named brothers and sisters and they elected new wardens, namely Walter Marchal through the pledge of John Gouky and William Morton through the pledge of John Glover. And they have in their keeping 21s. 4d.

And the said wardens rendered their accounts on the feast of St Botulph for the next year.

Let it be noted that on the Sunday after the feast of St. Botolph in the year AD 1411 William Marchal and William Morton wardens of the said Fraternity rendered their account in the presence of the above-named brothers and sisters and they elected new wardens, namely John Mankeswill through the pledge of John Gouky and William Balle through the pledge of Robert Goldehope and Richard Dewy and Walter Siffirwast. And they have in their keeping 22s. 4d.

Let it be noted that on the Sunday after the feast of St. Botolph in the 13 Henry IV [1412], John Mankeswill and William Balle wardens of the said Fraternity rendered their account in the presence of the above-named brothers and sisters and they elected new wardens, namely John Gouky through the pledge of William Marchall and Walter Siffirwast through the pledge of Nicholas Barbour. And they have in their keeping 25s. 1d.

Let it be noted that on the Sunday after the feast of St. Botolph in the 1 Henry V [1413], John Gouky and Walter Syffirwast, wardens of the said Fraternity rendered their account in the presence of the above-named brothers and sisters and they elected new wardens, namely John Gybbis through the pledge of Walter Siffirwast; and William Morton through the pledge of John Glover. And they have in their keeping 27s. 10d.

Let it be noted that on the Sunday after the feast of St. Botolph in the 3 Henry V [1415], William Morton and Adam Draper wardens of the said Fraternity rendered their account in the presence of the above-named brothers and sisters and they elected new wardens, William Morton and Adam Draper, and they have in their keeping 28s. And the aforesaid William found as a pledge William Marchall and the aforesaid Adam found as pledges William Morton and Walter Siffirwast, for the next day of accounts.

[page 6]
Let it be noted that on the Sunday after the Feast of the Purification of the Virgin Mary 14 Henry VI [1436], William Marchall and John Brode were elected wardens of the said Fraternity and they have in their keeping 12s. and the aforesaid William found as pledges Thomas Mankeswell and William Skynner, and the aforesaid John found as pledges John Mankeswell and Stephen Webbe and they must collect from John Sterre one pound of wax They received 16d. and they must collect from John Dyer 8d. Total sum 14s. and 1lb wax. And it was agreed that the accounts would be on the Sunday after the feast of St. Botulph.

Let it be noted that on the Sunday after the feast of St. Botolph 15 Henry VI [1437], William Marchall and John Brode wardens of the said Fraternity rendered their account in the presence of the above-named brothers and sisters and they elected new wardens, William Skynner and Walter Warde and they have in their keeping 15s.

2d. and the aforesaid William found as pledges William Marchall and John Brode and the aforesaid Walter found as pledges William Olyver and Thomas Mankeswell.

Let it be noted that on the Sunday after the feast of St. Botolph 16 Henry VI [1438], William Skynner and Walter Warde wardens of the said Fraternity rendered their account in the presence of the above-named brothers and sisters and they elected the same William and Walter through the above-named pledges and they have in their keeping 16s.

Let it be noted that on the Sunday after the feast of St. Botolph in the 17 Henry VI [1439], William Skynner and Walter Warde wardens of the said Fraternity rendered their account in the presence of the above-named brothers and sisters and they elected new wardens, Roger Daventre and John Mankeswell and they have in their keeping 16s. And the aforesaid Roger found as pledges William Olyver and John Brode and the aforesaid John found as pledges Thomas Mankeswell and William Skynner.

[page 7]
Let it be noted that on the Sunday after the feast of St. Botolph 18 Henry VI [1440], Roger Daventre and John Mankeswell wardens of the said Fraternity rendered their account in the presence of the above-named brothers and sisters and they elected the aforesaid Roger Daventre and John Mankeswell for the next year through the above-named pledges. And they have in their keeping 16s. 18s. 2d.

Let it be noted that on the Sunday after the feast of St. Botolph 22 Henry VI [1441], John Mankeswell and his colleague, wardens of the said Fraternity, rendered their account in the presence of the above-named brothers and sisters and they elected new wardens, John Sterre and William Olyver, and they have in their keeping 22s. 3d. And the aforesaid John found as pledges John Dyer and William Olyver and the aforesaid William Olyver found as pledges John Sterre and William House. John Boleyn junior received 9s. 4d. on behalf of John Sterre.

Let it be known that on the Sunday after the Feast which is known as St Peter ad Vincula in the 33rd year of the reign of Henry VI after the Conquest, John Sterre and William Olyver rendered their account, that is to say 19s. 4d. and they elected

Let it be known that on the Sunday after the Feast which is known as St Peter ad Vincula 33 Henry VI [1455], John Sterre and William Olyver, wardens of the aforesaid Fraternity, came and rendered their account in the presence of the above-named brothers and sisters, that is to say 19s. 4d., and they elected new wardens for the next year, namely William Howse through the pledge of William Olyver and John Newton, and Stephen Gregory through the pledge of John Boleyn junior. And William Howse received 9s. 8d. and Stephen Gregory received 9s. 8d. And the aforesaid Stephen fixed the date for the same John to pay the said Stephen 9s. 4d., on the Sunday after the feast of All Saints, to be well and faithfully observed by the same John, who touched the sacred Gospels in the presence of the aforesaid brothers and sisters.

[inside back cover] Watkin

**APPENDIX A:**

## THOMAS WAINWRIGHT'S TRANSLATION OF THE BOOK OF THE FRATERNITY OF THE LIGHT OF THE HOLY CROSS

The following text is a reproduction of Thomas Wainwright's handwritten translation (DC-BTB/PQ/28), made circa 1890, of a fifteenth century book, in Latin, in the Bridport Borough records (then ascribed the collection reference 2069). This book was not included in the documents later transferred to the Dorset History Centre in 1966. Therefore Wainwright's translation, together with a description included in the sixth report of the Royal Commission on Historical Manuscripts (see Appendix B) are the only surviving pieces of evidence for this lost book.

*Wainright's transcript of the book of The Fraternity of the Light of the Holy Cross*

[DC-BTB/PQ/28, page 96]

1399 – 1400
These are the names of the brethren and sisters of the fraternity of the light of the Holy Cross in the church of St Andrew at Brideport formed and commenced by the said brethren and sisters on Sunday next after the feast of the Epiphany of the Lord in the year 1399 for maintaining the light in the said church in honour of Our Lord Jesus Christ and of the Holy Cross and of his most holy mother and of all saints, namely:
William Scherard
John Tanner Joan his wife
Hugh Hyder, Alice his wife
John Mankeswill ~~Joan~~ Ellen his wife
Joan Mey, widow of William
Robert Leche, Emota his wife
Agnes Hore, widow of William
William Mey, Joan his wife
William Raffe, Christine his wife
John Stawman, Isabel his wife
Robert Abbot
Andrew Forsey, Florence his wife
Isabel Stalbryge
Hugh Hyder, Alice his wife
Christine Homan widow of John

Henry Raff, Alice his wife
John Crolle, Isabel his wife
Walter Chapman
John Bere, Joan his wife
Michell Phipps, Joan his wife
William Helyer, Joan his wife
Hugh Gendrig, Alice his wife
Robert Alchyn, Joan his wife
Thomas Stoke
Robert Gouldhop, Clarissa his wife
Alexander Trowet
Joan Hore, widow of Robert
John Borde
John Nythyng, Edith his wife
Ralph Tannere, Alice his wife
[page 97]
Avisia Dudenay
Robert Mattersale, Avice his wife
Edward Tracy, Margaret his wife
Peter Alchon, Eleanor his wife
Walter Amiel [or Amiet], Margaret his wife
William Curneis, Joan his wife
Peter Alchen, Elenor his wife
Thomas Roger, Alice his wife
William Curnes, Joan his wife
Stephen Davy, Joan / Marion
Thomas Roger, Alice his wife
Stephen Davy, Marion his wife
John Crosse, Alice his wife
Alice Crosse, widow of John
Willema wife of Nicholas Dunster
John Sterry, Lucy his wife
John Sterre and Lucy his wife
William Pernam, Lettice his wife
William Pernam, Lettice his wife
Nicholas Dunster, Willema his wife
Eleanor Hasard widow of John
Nicholas Dunster & Willema his wife
Richard Blampayn, Margaret his wife
John Burges, Agnes his wife
William Potel, Alice his wife, widow
William Marchel, Joan
Elizabeth Homan, widow of Roger
John Atkyn, Margaret his wife
Roger Dudeney, Avice his wife

John Clarke, Lucy his wife
John Chilterne, Alice his wife
William Tracy
Edward Tracy
Walter Annete, Margaret [*or Margery*] his wife

[page 98]
And be it remembered that it was thus ordained by the said brethren and sisters with unanimous consent, namely that

- On all Sundays and double festivals two candles shall be lighted at mass before the holy cross of the said light and it shall be renewed for the feast of the circumcision of the Lord.
- It was also ordained that all the brethren and sisters of the said fraternity shall come on the Sunday after the Epiphany of the Lord to the rendering of a faithful account of the common store by the appointed wardens.
- It was also ordained that all the brethren and sisters are to assemble together at the burial, vigil and masses on the day of the funeral of each brother and sister and if any one shall stay away, unless he has been hindered by a reasonable cause he shall pay half a pound of wax and each brother and sister shall deliver it to the wardens and cause a mass to be celebrated within a month for the soul of a deceased brother or sister.
- It was also ordained that if any one of the said fraternity shall depart this life anywhere [page 99] on land at a distance of seven miles from the parish of Bridport or shall be killed by an accident or by the perils of the sea, and his body has been found within the time named and he has bequeathed his body to be buried in the churchyards of St Mary, Bridport, that it shall be brought by the wardens of the said fraternity for interment where it can most conveniently be buried at the cost [of the estate] of the deceased if he has [left] property, otherwise at the expense of the said fraternity.
- It was also ordained that all the brethren and sisters shall accompany the corpse of the deceased to the church and each one of them shall offer at one mass one farthing.
- It was also ordained and allowed that if any brother or sister of the said fraternity come to such poverty that he has not the means of maintaining himself that he shall receive weekly from the wardens 3d or 4d or more that he may be maintained.
- Also each brother and sister shall come after sunset and shall say a Pater Noster and Ave Maria for the deceased brother or sister and there [page 100] at the expense [of the estate] of the deceased they shall drink once [*et ibidem sumptibus defuncti semel potare*] and there they shall remain until their names are marked
- The said brethren with the sisters with unanimous assent, touching God's holy gospels took their corporal oaths to keep and observe all and singular these ordinances and agreements in the aforesaid form.

Edward Traci, Margaret his wife

Roger Homan, Ulsot his wife
John Atkyn, Margaret his wife
John Forsey, Emota his wife
On Sunday after the feast of the Epiphany anno domini 1433 came the wardens of
the fraternity of the light of the holy cross in St Andrew's church at Brydport and
rendered their account and they elected new wardens for the year following, namely
John Nything, Edward Tracy, and William Myllward being his sureties and John Peers
alias Atkyn with John Forsey and Stephen Davy as sureties and each of these wardens
received 37s 7½d. Total £3 15s 3d. Be it remembered that 2lbs of wax are in the hands
of John Sterre.
[page 101]
Nicholas Skynner
William Ros
William Swayn
William Preder [it appears Wainright has misread the letter Þ for a capital P and that
this surname was pronounced Threder], towker [*i.e. tucker*]
Edward Tracy
Stephen Davy
John Atkyn
John Burges
William Marchel
Isabel Stalbryge
John Forsey
Memorandum 2s 7d remaining in the hands of the wardens paid to the clerk for his
work
Thomas Baker, Christine his wife, 10d
Richard Cause, Joan his wife, 10d
Thomas Stocfysh, Agnes his wife, 10d
John Hylle 12d
William House 12d
John Forsey, Emmot his wife
Joan wid William Myllward
John Hyder, Margaret his wife
John Mankeswill, Emot his wife
John Harrys, Sara his wife
John Crypse, Edith his wife
Ralph Vynsent, Alice / Agnes (sic) his wife
William Olyver, Joan his wife
Thomas Baker, Christine his wife
Richard Cause, Joan his wife
Thomas Stokfysh, Agnes his wife
John Hylle, Joan his wife
William House, Alice his wife
John Boleyn junior, Alice his wife

[page 102]
Thomas Wey, Joan his wife
John Teymoth, Agnes his wife
Walter Payne, Florence his wife
John Downe, Edith his wife
William Bremlegh, Isabel his wife
John Mate, Matilda his wife
Andrew Mannyng, Margaret his wife
Nicholas Hore, Alice his wife
John Dunne, Emota his wife
John Perys junior, Agnes his wife
William Wodewale, Mabel his wife
Walter Smyth alias Graunson, Margaret his wife
John Trycaldy, Agnes his wife
John Bytesgate junior, Joan his wife
Richard Burgh, Alice
Thomas Porter and Alice his wife
Thomas Clerke and Margaret his wife paid 6d
1400. On Sunday after the Epiphany of our Lord in the 1st year of King Henry II
[*presumably an error for Henry IV*] came Walter Chepman and William Stork and paid in
to the fund to the said brethren of the said fraternity £3 7s 0d and new wardens were
elected namely William Mey and John Homan, butcher.
Of the said £3 7s 0d
William Mey received 34s 6d, surety Henry Tite
John Homan, butcher 34s 6d, surety Hugh Hyde
[*Note: the receipts are greater than the total*]

[page 103-105]
On the Sunday after the Epiphany

|  | Old Wardens | Paid in | New Wardens | Sureties |
|---|---|---|---|---|
| 1400 | John Homan | £3 14s 0d | William Mey | Andrew Forsey |
|  | William Mey |  | Adam Hasard | Henry Tite |
| 1402 | William Mey | £3 18s 0d | William Colmoure | Hugh Hyder and John Pryoure |
|  | Adam Hasard |  | Nicholas Skynner | |
|  |  |  |  | William Willyam of Mangerton |
| 1403 | William Colmoure | £4 6s 0d | William Swayn | Robert Alchyn |
|  | Nicholas Skynner |  | Nicholas Skynner | William Coke of Mangerton |
| 1404 | William Swayn | £4 19s 0d | William Swayn | William Touker |
|  | Nicholas Skynner |  | Nicholas Skynner | William Koc of Mangerton |
| 1405 | William Swayn | £5 2s 0d | William Mey | John Homan, boucher |
|  | Nicholas Skynner |  | Nicholas Skynner | Roger Bron |

| | | | | |
|---|---|---|---|---|
| 1406 | William Mey<br>Nicholas Skynner | £5 8s 0d | Adam Hasard<br>Wm. Colmour | Andrew Forsey<br>John Pryour |
| 1407 | Adam Hasard<br>William Colmour | £3 11s 0d | William Colmour<br>William Swayne | Hugh Hyder<br>William Threder |
| 1408 | William Colmour<br>William Swayne | £3 14s 8d | Thomas Goky<br>William Ball | William Raaf<br>Adam Hasard [page 104] |
| 1409 | Thomas Gouky<br>William Balle | £3 18s 0d | William Balle<br>Gilbert Peverell | Adam Hasard<br>John Homan |
| 1410 | William Balle<br>Gilbert Peverell | £4 6s 4d | Adam Draper<br>William Swayne | John Pryour<br>Walter Annes |
| 1411 | Adam Draper<br>William Swayne | £4 6s 4d | Adam Draper<br>William Balle | Henry Tyte<br>Thomas Gouky |

And William Swayne received from the said brethren 24s, sureties John Shippe, prior of St John, and John Bere

| | | | | |
|---|---|---|---|---|
| 1412 | Adam Draper<br>William Balle | £4 13s 0d | Andrew Forsay<br>Henry Raw | Thomas Goky<br>John Prior |
| 1413 | Andrew Forsay<br>Henry Raw | £4 12s 0d | William Mey<br>William Balle | Andrew Forshay<br>Nicholas Barber |

Be it remembered that Andrew Forshey delivered to William Mey of Brudeford 36s. John Homan and John Prior being sureties on the said account day. [page 105]

| | | | | |
|---|---|---|---|---|
| 1414 | William Mey<br>William Balle | £3 12s 0d | Thomas Gouky<br>John Pawe | W.<br>Henry Tyte |
| 1415 | Thos Gouky<br>John Pawe | £3 14s 6d | William Marchell<br>Thomas Roger | Henry Tite<br>Roger Brone |
| 1416 | William Marchell<br>Thos Roger | £3 14s 6d | William Marchell<br>Thos Roger | Henry Tyte<br>Robert Stalbrigge |
| 1417 | William Marchell<br>Thomas Roger | £3 10s 0d | Thomas Gouky<br>Robt Alschon | Walter Sifferwest, John Prioure and John Homan |
| 1418 | Thomas Gouky<br>Robert Alschon | £3 15s 0d | Thomas Gouky<br>Robert Alschon | Walter Sifferwest, John Prioure and John Homan |
| 1419 | Thomas Gouky<br>Robert Alschon | £3 10s 8d | John Prior<br>John Croshe | Thomas Gouky, Henry Tyte and William. Marchell |
| 1420 | John Prior<br>John Crosh | £3 6s 8d | Hugh Hyde<br>John Homan | William Hore and Nicholas Piris, William Marchell and William Goky |
| 1421 | Hugh Hude<br>John Homan | £3 8s 0d | Nicholas Piris<br>Stephen Davy | Wm. Marchell and Henry Tyte, John Prior and John Crosse |

[page 106]
The entries are continued as before until the 2nd year of the reign of Henry VII, 1487, the expression "*Reddiderunt in stauro in pecunia munera*" they paid in counted money

frequently occurs. The amounts paid varied little from the preceding, rising however to £4 10s 6d in 1428 and dropping to 57s 4d in 1456, a frequent amount is £4 1s 0d. There are no entries between 39 Henry VI and 13 Edward IV, 1461 – 1474.

After the entry of the year 1429 is written the following,
These are the names of the brethren of the fraternity of the Holy Cross in St Andrew's church at Brideport now deceased:
John Mankeswille
John Tannere, Joan his wife
Joan Webbe
Isabel wife of Robert Leche
Michael Philyppe
Joan wife of Henry Raff
Roger Gay
Matilda [and] Christine wives of Gilbert Peverell
John Irlonde
William Irlonde
Elizabeth wife Walter Chepman
William Tynkelder
Alice wife Robert Abbot
Thomas Elmys
Ralph Tannere
Joan wife of John Priour
Florence wife of Robert Abbot
Alice wife of William Row

[page 107]
After the account of 18 Henry VI, 1440, the following is entered:
And the said wardens are required to mend the room [?] with (*inserted above:* cum = and?) the window shutter under a penalty of 12d for the two of them.

After 20 Henry VI, 1442
And the said wardens received 2 lbs of wax from John Boleyn and pay it into the store

After 28 Henry VI, 1450
And the said wardens were charged with the fine of John Dun  8d
And the said wardens were charged with 2 lbs of wax, the fine of  John Tengmothe
And the said wardens were charged with [blank],the fine of William Wodewale

After 29 Henry VI, 1451
And the said wardens were charged with the fine of John Dun  8d
And the said wardens were charged with 2 lbs of wax, the fine of Robert Downe

After 30 Henry VI, 1452
As above, the said wardens were charged with the fine of Nicholas Hore and John

Mate 18d
The said wardens were charged with the fine of John Trygalty 2 lbs of wax or 12d

[page 108]
After 33 Henry VI, 1455
Total £4 12d
Whereof 26s 8d was delivered to William Olyver to buy two large antiphonaries, namely "lyggers" [*ledgers*] for the use of St Mary's church and so there remains in the hands of the said wardens 54s 4d.

After 35 Henry VI, 1457
And the said wardens are charged to collect mass money for the souls of John Atkyn and Emot Dun by the anniversary. Also they are charged to repair the stairs and [blank space] under a penalty of 40d to be paid to the the light of the Holy Cross of St Andrews

After 37 Henry VI, 1459
Also the said wardens received from John Sterre 4d and from Joan Dune 4d for mass money for the souls of John Attekyn, Emota Dunne, Joan Marshall and John Forsey.

After 38 Henry VI, 1460
Also the said wardens were charged with 6d or one lb of wax from the fine of Walter Smyth, but [page 109] the said Walter was not willing to pay the said 6d and we the said brethren and sisters determined that he should be expelled from our fraternity.

After 13 Edward IV, 1474
Also John Tengmouthe promised to pay to the said wardens 3s 4d next Easter and each term of that year 20d towards a sum of 16s 8d which he owes to the said fraternity.

After 14 Edward IV, 1475
Also the wardens were charged to receive from Richard Burgh 1lb of wax.

After 15 Edward IV, 1476
Also the wardens were charged to secure from Richard Burgh 1lb of wax, paid Robert Hylle for 1lb of wax, paid William Rakerayne for 1lb of wax, paid William Scheter for 1lb of wax

After 16 Edward IV, 1477
1lb of wax from John Tengmouthe, 10s
For the fine of William Stikylpathe, 6d
The fine of Richard Burgh, 6d

[page 110]
After 17 Edward IV, 1478
Also the wardens were charged to receive from John Tengmowthe 10s *viz.* 2s 6d each

term

After 18 Edward IV, 1479
For the fine of William Taylor, 6d
For the fine of William Christopher, 6d
For the fine of John Frankelyne, 6d
For the fine of John Sanford, 6d
For the debt of John Tengmowthe, 10s
For the fine of Rich Burgh's wife , 6d

After 19 Edward IV, 1480
For the fine of John Sanford, 6d
For the fine of William Christopher, 6d
For the fine of William Tayler, 6d
And to receive from John Tengmowthe 2d every Sunday in the year until the sum of
10s is paid.

After 21 Henry VI [*error for Edward IV*], 1482
To receive 2d per week every Sunday from John Tengmowthe until the debt of 5s is
paid.

[page 111]
After 2 Richard III, 1485
The wardens were charged to receive from the fine of John Croford, 6d
Walter Colmer was elected a brother, fine 1lb of wax, 6d
From Richard Keche and Joan his wife 1 lb of wax, 6d

After 1 Henry VII, 1486
For the fine of Richard Whytehorne, 1lb of wax
For the fine of John Kent, 1lb of wax
For the fine of Thomas Elasander, 1lb of wax

After 2 Henry VII, 1487
For the fine of John Hasard, 6d

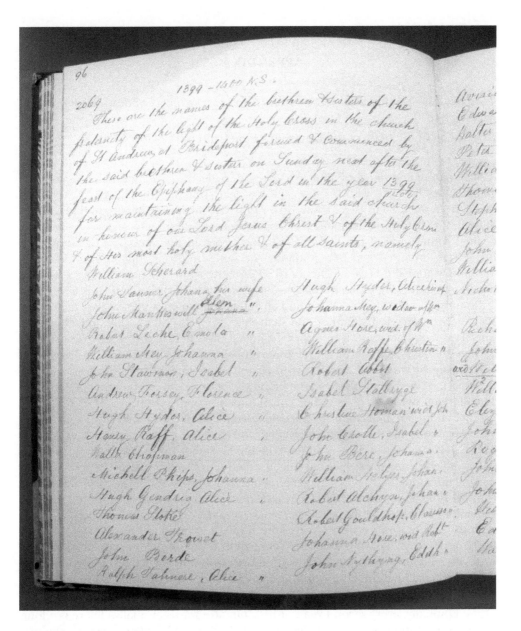

*DC-BTB/PQ/28: Wainwright's transcription of the lost book of the Fraternity of the Light of the Holy Cross.*

## APPENDIX B.

*The sixth report of the Royal Commission on Historical Manuscripts* (London, HMSO, 1877), pages 178-9.

Description of the book of the Fraternity of the Light of the Holy Cross.

A small parchment book, of about 40 leaves, duo- decimo size, bound in, apparently, goat-leather, fastened with a strap. The first leaf contains a list of names, the date being, from the second page, about A.D. 1434. The third page begins, in fine writing, in Latin, — " These are the names of the brethren and their fellow sisters (*consororum*) of the Brotherhood of the Light of the Holy Cross, in the church of St. Andrew of Brudeport, ordained and begun among the same brethren and their fellow-sisters on Sunday after the Feast of Our Lord's Epiphany 1399 "for maintaining a light in the church aforesaid; to the honour of Our Lord Jesus Christ, and of Holy Cross, and of his most Blessed Mother, Mary, and all Saints." The names then follow, headed by William Scherard, John Tanner and Joan, his wife, John Mankeville and Elena, his wife. Two wax tapers are to be kept burning at Mass, before the cross, every Sunday and on double Feasts. Those of the Fraternity who die within one mile of Brideport, or are slain or disowned at sea, are to be buried in the churchyard of St. Mary of Brideport. At the burial, all the members, at the Mass, are to offer, each, one farthing. The like sum per week is also to be contributed for poor brethren and sisters. Every brother and sister shall come (to the church) after sunset, and shall say "Paternoster" and "Ave Maria" for the member deceased; and shall there have one drink, at the cost of the deceased (et ibidem, sumptibus defuncti, semol potare) and there they are to stay until their names shall have been called. On the 7th leaf there is some little musical notation, in two parts; a fragment, in a hand, probably, of the close of the 14th century. It begins abruptly "tu scez bien de qeor, verra qe jeo teyme damour entiere: (next line) ferrai tant cum viverai, ne ja men irray arere" ("thou knowest well at heart, shalt see that I love thee with " love entire: I will do so long as I live, nor ever will go back therefrom)." Below is written, "Tenor de A toute here," " Tenor in A, always." Unfortunately the music has been written over with a list of names; though, after a prolonged examination, both words and notation might perhaps be made out.

The accounts were given in, and new Wardens chosen, on Sunday after the Feast of the Epiphany, every second year, at first, but afterwards annually. There is a long hiatus in the entries of accounts given in and elections of Wardens, between the first and the 13th year of Edward IV [1461-1474]. The latest entry is of the 2nd year of Henry VII [1487].

## APPENDIX C.

*Fragmentary pages from a copy of the Customary of Sarum, used as a binding to the records of the Fraternity of the Light Hanging before the Cross (CD11).*

### CD11 - 3
*(lh column)*
...form. On weekdays within the octave of Ascension Day, the first antiphon is sung in the first form; the second and third in the second form; the lessons and responsories as on other weekdays. At lauds, it is as on the lesser single feasts on which the choir is ruled, in their own season. However on Sundays within octaves the manner and order of service should be observed which is proper to other Sundays, except for those things that are excluded in the rosters of the Sunday masses.

On feasts of three lessons when the choir is not ruled and on every memorial of the Blessed Virgin, the manner and order should be observed as on weekdays in all respects, except that on certain such feasts and on the memorials of the Blessed Virgin, the invitatory should be sung by two.

Feasts on which the Invitatory is sung by two.

St Julian, bishop and confessor

Agn[es] ....St Blaise .......

(rest of column illegible)

*(rh column)*
... Crescentia, Vitus and Modestus. Marcus and Marcellianus, martyrs. Gervasius and Prothasius, martyrs. The Translation of St Edward. John and Paul.

In the month of August: St Stephen, pope and martyr. Oswald, king and martyr. Sixtus, Felicissimus and Agapitus. St Tiburtius, martyr. Within the octave of St Lawrence... Hippolytus, martyr. Rufinus, martyr.... Felix and Adauctus. St Cuthberga, virgin, not a martyr. In the month of September: the Translation of St Cuthbert. SS Cypriana and Justina. SS Cosmo and Damian, martyrs. In the month of October: Marcus and Marcellus and Apuleius. Nigasius and his companions. Calixtus, pope and martyr. The Eleven Thousand Virgins. Crispin and Crispinian, martyrs. In the month of November: the Holy Crowned Martyrs. Brice, bishop and confessor. St Anianus, bishop. The octave of St Martin and any service of commemoration within an octave. Similarly for St Andrew. In the month of December: the octave of St Andrew.

The manner of blessing the water on the first Sunday of Advent and on the other Sundays...

**CD11- 4**

*(lh column)*

the duty priest for the week, along with a deacon and subdeacon holding the Text and a boy holding the thurible and candlebearers and an acolyte holding the cross, all vested in albs and turned to face the altar in the middle of the presbytery, shall make the holy water at the choir step: and the boy who is down for water duty in the roster shall, wearing a surplice, assist the priest, by holding the salt while the water is blessed and carrying the holy water: and the boy on duty for the week for reading at matins shall, wearing a surplice, assist the priest by holding the book.

Of the sprinking of holy water

The blessing completed, the priest himself should approach the principal altar and sprinkle it on every side: returning he should first sprinkle his assistants in the order given, starting with the acolyte: then returning to the choir step, he should sprinkle each of the clerics who should come up to him at that same place, starting with the most senior. However if the bishop is present, the aspersion of the clerics falls to him. After the aspersion of the clerics, he should sprinkle the laymen standing on either side in the presbytery. Once the aspersion of the holy water has been completed, the priest should return to the choir step and there say the prayer with the versicle.

*(rh column)*

then the rest follow in the order aforesaid, then the boys and those from the second form in the order in which they placed in the choir: the rest from the upper step in the same order as they are placed in the chapter, without changing their vestments. However, the bishop – if he should be present – shall wear his mitre and carry his staff: and the procession should leave through the north presbytery door, and go around the presbytery. The priest should asperse each altar in passing: then the procession going down the south side of the Cathedral, should come by way of the font and proceed to a place before the cross; and there, they should make a station, the priest and his aforementioned ministers standing in the middle in order; and in this way, that the boy carrying the water and the acolyte should stand on the step in front of the cross: then, when the customary prayers have been said, they should enter the choir, and the priest should say the versicle and prayer at the choir step: then he should go with his ministers to asperse the canons' cemetery, praying for the dead.

The adaptation of the procession on this Sunday for the other Sundays with their exceptions.

This manner and order of procession should generally be observed on every ordinary Sunday throughout the year. However, on the Sundays from Septuagesima to Quadragesima

**CD11- 23**

*(lh column)*

in the second form by the first cleric of that level; and while he starts he should stand turned to face the choir: but at the end of the first verse of the psalm he should bow to the altar; and this turning and bowing should also be generally observed throughout the year, whatever rank of cleric begins the antiphon. The other antiphons following should run in this way along both sides. This manner for starting these antiphons should be observed on every Saturday throughout the year. After the third psalm three boys should, after getting permission from the rulers of the choir, go out in order to robe themselves, two for taking the candles, the third the thurible. And the priest saying the chapter should change neither his stall nor his vestment but, saying it, should turn to face the altar: and this should always be observed. At these vespers two clerics from the upper step, wearing silken copes, should sing at the choir step: the responsory should be sung at vespers in the same way on the Saturdays before Passion Sunday and Palm Sunday: but on the other Saturdays throughout the year, when the service is from the Temporal and a responsory is to be sung, it is to be sung by two from the second form, in silken copes. During the penultimate verse of the hymn.....

*(rh column)*

...to put on a silken cope. Once the hymn has been said, one boy from the duty side of the choir should say the versicle, turned towards the altar but without changing either his position or vestment. The same manner should be observed by any boy who sings a versicle or Benedicamus by himself. In the meantime, the candlebearers should come in, and, having taken up the candlesticks, go to meet the priest at the presbytery step. Then the priest should put the incense into the thurible, blessing it, and proceed to the altar; and after genuflecting before the altar, he should cense it, first in the middle, then on the right side, afterwards the left; next the image of the Blessed Virgin, and afterwards the chest in which the relics are contained: then he should go round the altar, censing; having done this, the priest should go to the last step before the altar and bow towards the altar: and, with the candlebearers and the thurible going before him, he should take his place in the stall assigned to this office. Of the censing of the choir. Then a boy censes the priest himself: afterwards, the rulers of the choir, starting with the principal ruler, then those on the upper step, on the side....

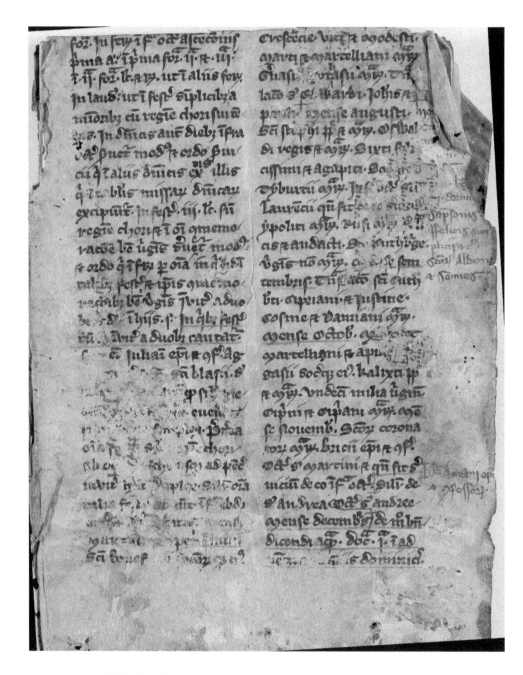

*DC-BTB/CD/11: section of the customary of Sarum recycled as book binding.*

# INDEX

Ablee (Able), John, 42, 59-61
  Eleanor, 42
Adam, Richard, 34
Akerman, Stephen, 60
Alchen (Alchon, Alchyn, Alchyne), Eleanor, 79
  Joan, 14, 79
  John, 7
  Peter, 3, 7, 14, 21, 32, 79
  Robert, 3, 14, 79, 82
ales, xviii-xix, xxviii, xxxi, 39-40, 55-9, 62
Algar (Algare), John, 33, 42, 45-6
  Lucy, 42
Allington, xiv-xv, xxi-xxii
alms, xv
Alschon, Robert, 83
Amiel (Amiet), Margaret, 79
  Walter, 79
Andrew, Hugh, 40
Annes, Walter, 83
Annette, Walter, 80
antiphonaries (music books or ledgers), xxii, xxxix, xliv, 1, 45, 90
Arundell, John, 55
Atkyn (Attekyn, Atkynne), John, xxxiv, xxxix, 4, 10-11, 43, 79, 81, 85
  Margaret, xxxiv, 4, 10-11, 43, 79, 81
  Nicholas, 22, 26, 29
Atlington, 24
Atram, 58, 60
Atwere (atte Weer, Attewere, Atweere), John, 33, 38
Atwey, Hugh, 60
Axeminster (Axemenster), Richard de, 71
Axemouth (de Axemouth), Joan, 49-50-2
  John, 50-2
Axmoth, Robert, 72
Ayleward, Joan, 4
  Robert, 4
Ayleworth, Emmota, 22

William, 22
Aylmund, Stephen, 69-71

bailiff(s), bailiffs, xiii-xiv, xxxiii, xxxv, xxxix, xl, 1, 11-12, 50-5, 64-7, 70, 72
Baker (Bakere), Christine, 81
  Henry (Harry), 14, 21-2
  James, 29
  Joan, 14, 21, 32-3
  Nicholas, 59
  Thomas, 14, 81
  William, 54
Baktom, John, 40
Ball (Bal, Balle), William, 72, 74-5, 83
Barber (Barbor, Barbour), Joan, 21, 72
  Nicholas, 21, 32-3, 72, 74-5, 83
barley, 50
Bath and Wells, bishop of, xiv
Batyn, Richard, 62
Bawdyn, John, 62
Bayly (Bayley), Margery, 4, 47
  Thomas, 1, 4, 10, 47, 61, 65
beans, 50
beer, see also ales, xxx-xxxi, 29, 57-8
Beese, John, 4
Beminster, Alice, xxxii, 42
Benefeld (Benesfeld), Joan, xxxii, 51-3
  John, 51-3
Benegir, Nicholas, 72
Benett (Benet), John, 43
  Thomas, 33, 38-9
Bere (Beer, Ber), Joan, 79
  John, xxxix, 26, 79, 83
Beres, Lucy, 32
Berteram (Bertram), Alice, 43
  James, 43, 46-8
Bestelawe (Bestelaw, Bestlawe), Agnes, 32
  Joan, 3
  John, 32, 34-6
  William, 3, 5

Beverley, Mary, xviii
Bevyn, John, 54
    William, 71
Bexington, Walter, 21
Beymynster (Bemyster), Robert, 50-2
Binne, William, 11-12
Bittesgate (Byttelisgate, Bittelisgate,
        Bytesgate, Bittisgate), Joan, 33, 82
    John, xxxix, 33, 82
    Richard, 64-5
Blampayn, Margaret, 79
    Richard, 79
Bodmin (Cornwall), fraternities at, xvi
Bokerell, John, 56, 60
Bolyn (Boleyne, Bolyne, Bulleyn), Alice, 33,
        73, 81
    Joan, 60
    John, xxxi, xxxviii, 33-4, 38, 61, 73, 76,
        81, 84
Bonvyld, Henry, 56
Borage, Agnes, xxxiv, 4, 42
    John, xxxiv, 4, 6-7, 16, 42-4
    William, 54-5
Borde, John, 79
Bouche (Bowche, Buche), Thomas, 22, 27-9
    Thomasina, 22
Bowdych (Boudich), Isabel, 72
    John, 3, 72
Bowge (Bouge), Thomas, 26-7
Bowley (Bouley, Bowsley), Adam, 72
    Christiane, 12, 42, 72
    William, 12, 16-17, 35-6, 40, 42-5, 49
Bracy, Robard, 62
Brangewayne (Bradwyne, Brangwayn,
        Brangwayne, Brangwaynger), Joan, 14
    Richard, 3, 5-7, 14-17, 43-5
Brasyheter, Alice, 3
bread, xxx-xxxi, 29, 56-8
Brekefast, Agnes, 21
Breman, John, 39
Bremell (Bremyll), Alice, xxxiii, 33, 65
    John, 33, 54, 56, 60-1, 65
Bremlegh, Isabel, 82
    William, 82
Bret, Robert, 3
Brice, Nicholas, 55
Bridgwater, hospital at, 53
Bridport, agreements made in borough
        court, 1, 11

Asker bridge, xxii
    barn, 56, 66-7
    bars, 69-70
    Blindelane, 11
    bridges, xxxiii, 71
    burgage plots, xiii, xxxiii, 54-5, 66
    burgesses, xiii-xv, xxxiii, 66
    castle, xii
    chantries, xii, xiv-xv, xxi-xxiii, xxxv-xxxvi,
        xxxix, xliii
    Church Lane, 64
    church of Saint Andrew, 71, 88
    church of Saint Mary, x, xiii, xxii, xliv, 1,
        3, 10-12, 18, 45, 64, 81, 84
    churchyard, 18, 80, 88
    Culverhay, 56
    dovecot, 52
    East Bridge, xiv, xxxiii
    East Street, xxii, xxxii-xxxiii, 53
    Frerynorchard, 56
    harbour, xiv-xv, xl
    hospital of St John (leper hospital), xiv
    hospital of St Mary Magdalen, xiv, xxi
    Irish Lane (Irysche Lane), xxxiii, 66
    Killyngeslane, 49-52
    mill, 66
    Munden's chantry, xiv, xxi, xxxiii, xxxv,
        xxxix, xliii, 65
    Nicholas of 15, 16, 17, 40
    rector of, xvii, xxxvi, xxxixxiv,
    rents, 12, 49, 51-7, 60, 64-8, 70-2, 74
    St Andrew's Chapel, xiv, xxii, xxxix, 67,
        70-2
    St Katherine's Chantry, 51-4
    St Mary Magdalen's Chantry, xxi
    St Michael's Lane, xxxiii, 56, 65
    salt pans, 55, 58, 60
    Snawdon (Snawedon), 49-51
    South Street, xii-xiv, xxii, xxxii-xxxiii, 11,
        53, 66, 69-70
    tower, 71
    town ditch, xl
    West Street, xiii, xxii, xxxii
Bristol, 71
Brode, Alice, 4, 14, 33, 73
    John, xxx, 4, 6-9, 14-17, 21-9, 33-6, 73,
        75-6
    Margaret, 21
Brone (Bron), Roger, 82-3

Browne, Edith, 42
    John, 61
    William, 61
Brownyng, Thomas, 66
BrownysJoan, xxxiv, 59
Budde, Robert, 50, 52
Bure, Laurence, 52
Burges (Borges, Burge, Burgeis, Burgess,
        Burgeys, Burgeyse, Burgys), Amisia, 14
    Joan, 32
    John, xxxiv, 7-11, 14, 16-17, 43-5, 49, 79,
        81
    Robert, 21-5, 32
    William, 62
Burgh, Agnes, 33, 42, 54
    Alice, 48, 54
    Joan, 33, 45, 48, 62
    John, xxxiii, 54-5
    Margaret, 42
    Marion, 54
    Richard, 33, 37-9, 42-8, 54, 59, 61-2, 65,
        67, 82, 85
    Robert, 33, 39, 42, 45, 48, 54, 61
burial, see fraternities,
butcher, xxxv, 4, 82
Butte (But, Butt, Buttes), Alice, 4
    Emota, xxxix, 25
    Joan, 49
    John, xxxix, 5-6, 16-17, 32, 34-6, 42-5, 66
    Roger, 64
    William, 12, 72
Byconell, John, 54
Bylke, John, 61

Cabyn, John, 72
Calwell, Walter, 4
candlebearers, 90-1
candles, see also lights, torches and wax, xvii,
        xix, xxi-xxiii, xxvi, xxviii, xxxi, 18, 25,
        32, 40, 56, 73-
4, 80, 91
Cardmaker, Nicholas, 64
carpenter, xxxv, 73
Causy (Cause, Cawsy), Richard, 22, 24-5, 81
chantries, see Bridport, xxi
Chapel, see St Andrew's Chapel,
chaplain, Richard, the, 56
chaplains, xiv, xviii, xxxii-xxxiii, xxxvi, xxxix,
        42, 48, 52-6, 70

Chapman (Chepman), Walter, 79, 82, 84
chapmen, xxxv
charity, see also poverty/poor relief, xix-xx
Cherde (Charde), Thomas, 46-8, 54-5, 65
    William, 66
Chester, Helen, 21
    Richard, 21
Chilterne, Alice, 80
    John, 80
choir, see also music and singing, 91
Christopher, William, 86
churchwardens, xvii, xxxv
Chydeock (Chideoc, Chydeocke, Chydyock,
        Chydyocke, Chydyok, de Chidiok),
        Florence, 3
    John, 3-4, 7-8, 50-1
    Nicholas de, xxxii, 12
Chylteryn, John, 3
Chynne, Richard, 69
Clement, Emma, 33
    John, 33
Clenche, William, 21
Clerk (Clarke, Clerke), Henry, 72
    John, 80
    Lucy, 80
    Margaret, 82
    Robert, 72
    Thomas, 62, 72, 82
    Walter, 73
Cobbe, John, 60
Cock, Alexander, 21, 50
cofferer, of the borough, 53
        of the fraternity of St Katherine, 53-4
        of the fraternity of the Holy Trinity, 68
Coke, William, 82
Cole, Thomas, 50
Colmer (Colmour, Colmoure), Walter, 86
    William, 54, 82-3
Colt, William, 11, 12
Colwylle, Walter, 32
Cordal (Cordaill), William, 50, 53
Corle (Corell), John, 23-6
Cornysche (Cornysh), Joan, xxxiii, 64
    William, 56, 61, 64
Cottell, John, 66
Couk, Alice, 73
    Thomas, 73
    William, 73
Coukys, Joan, 21

Cowley, Robert, 64
craft guilds, xvi
Crewys, John, 61
Crips (Cripce, Cripse, Cryps, Crypse),
    Custans, 48
   Edith, 42, 48
   John, 42, 45-6, 48, 60-1, 81
Crocker (Crokker), Edith, 33
   William, 33, 38-9, 59-60
Croford, John, 86
Crokehorne (Crokern, Crokhorne,
    Crowkern, Krokorne), John, 56, 60
   William, 50-3
Crolle (Croll, Crull, Crulle), Isabel, xxxiv,
    29, 79
   John, xxxiv, 21-2, 24-9, 79
Crosh (Croshe), John, 83
Crosse, Alice, 42, 79
   John, xxii, 42, 79, 83
Cukeroyl, Peter, 11
Cunteryman, John, 60
Curle, John, 24
Curneis (Curnes), Joan, 79
   William, 79
Custumary of Sarum, xliv, 89, 92
Cute, John, 12

Dannur, Thomas, 12
Davage, Richard, 66-7
Davelle (Davell, Davyle), Edith, 21
   Richard, 21, 25-9
Daventre (Davynter, Davyngtre, Dawynter,
    Dowentre), Joan, 3, 14, 73
   Roger, 3, 5-6, 14, 73-4, 76
Davy (Davey, Davi, Dawey), Gregory, 72
   Joan, 14, 32, 72, 79
   Marion, 79
   Stephen, xxxix, 14, 16-17, 32, 34-8, 40,
    79, 81, 83
deacon, 90
Deighr, Richard, 21
Denslow, John, 58
Dewy, Alice, 73
   Richard, 73-5
Deycoke, Alice, 21
   Thomas, 21
Do, John, 21
Doget, John, 62
Dolle (Dol), Agnes, 21

   John, 14
Dorchester, Fraternity at, xxi
Douke (Dowke), Alice, 33
   Clarice, 72
   John, 72
   Richard, 72
   William, 33
Down (Downe), Edith, 82
   John, 9, 82
   Robert, 84
Drake, Thomas le, 70
   Walter, 12
Draper, Adam, 75, 83
   Alice, 32
Dudeney, Avice, 79
   Roger, 79
Dunne (Dun), Emota, 4, 82, 85
   Joan, 85
   John, 4, 9-10, 59-60, 64-5, 67-8, 82, 84
Dunster, Nicholas, 79
   Willema, 79
Dyer (Deyr), Christine, 73
   John, 60, 62, 73, 75-6
dyers, xxxv
Dymmet, John, 60

Edmunde, William, xxxix, 61
Edward, John, 53-4
Elasander (Elasaunder), Thomas, 53, 86
Ellewill (Elwyll), Hilbrond 55, 57
Elmys, Thomas, 84
Elyce, William, 64
Elynoth, Laurence, 11
Englysch, William, 56
Esse (Eysse), Clement de 70-1
Exemouth, John, 51

Ferthyng, Richard, 52
fishermen, xxxv
Flete, Thomas, 61
Forde, Agnes at, 21, 42
   Simon at, 42
   Thomas at 21, 42
Forde Abbey (Somerset), xxxiii
Forsay (Forsey, Forshay, Forshey), Andrew 78,
    82-3
   Emma, 49
   Emmota, 43, 81
   Florence, 78

Isabel, 78

John, 35-8, 40, 43, 81, 85

Frankelyne, John, 86

Fraternities, annual meal, xxx, 29

    Burials of members, xiv, xvi-xix, xxi, xxvi,
        4, 14-15, 18, 32, 40, 73-4, 80, 88

    elections of officers and members, xiii,
        xxviii-xxix, xxxiv-xxxv, xliii-xliv

    offices and office holders (see also
        bailiffs, cofferers, stewards, wardens),
        xii, xviii-xxi, xxvi-

xxx, xli, xlvi

    ordinances, xviii-xix, xxiii, xxvi-xxx, xli,
        xliv

Fraternity of St George (Wymondham,
    Norfolk), xix

Fraternity of St John, xxii

Fraternity of St Katherine, xxxi-xxxvi, xxxix-
    xl, 1, 42-55

Fraternity of St Mary and St James, xxii, xxiv-
    xxvii, xxx, xxxiv-xxxviii, xli, xliii, 72-7

Fraternity of St Nicholas, xxiii, xxvi, xxix-xxx,
    xxxv-xxxviii, xlii-xliii, 12-18

Fraternity of St Swithin, xxii, xliv

Fraternity of St Thomas, xxii

Fraternity of the Blessed Virgin Mary, xxviii-
    xxix, xxxi, xxxiv-xxxvi, xxxviii-xxxix,
    xli, xliii, 1, 55-67

Fraternity of the Holy Cross, xxii, xxiv, xxvi,
    xxviii, xxxv-xli, 1, 67-8

Fraternity of the Holy Trinity, xxii, xxiv, xxxi,
    xxxiii, xxxvi, xli, xliii, 68-72

Fraternity of the Light Hanging Before the
    Cross, xxii, xxvi, xxxiv, xxxvii, xliv, 3-10,
    78-88

Fraternity of the Mortuary Lights, xxix, xxxi-
    xxxiii, 11-12

Fraternity of the Torches, xxii, xxvi, xxix-xxx,
    xxxiv, xxxvi-xxxvii, xliv, 18-32

Fraternity of the Two Torches, xxiii, xxvi,
    xxviii-xxix, xxxv, xxxviii-xxxix, xlv, 32-
    42

Freman, William, 32

Fulford, Humphrey, 54

funerals, see fraternities,

Funtell (Fontell), Agnes, 22, 33

    William, 22, 28-9, 33, 35-6, 38

Furber, Philip, 60

Fyce, John, 60

Gamelyn (Gamelyne), Agnes, xxxiv, 22

    Henry, xxxiv, 42-45, 49

    Joan, 21, 42, 45

    William, 22, 24-7

Garnet, Henry, 71

Gendon, William, 64

Gervays, John, 12

Gillingham, Fraternity at, xxi

Glendrig, Alice, 79

    Hugh, 79

Glover, John, 74-5

glover, 72

Gokey (Goky, Gouky), John, 73-5

    Stephen, 59-60

    Thomas, 83

    William, 83

Goldsmith (Goldsmyth), John, 50-1

Gollop, Clare, 72

    Robert, 72, 74

    William, 72

Golofre, Adam, 12

Goly, daughter of 62

Gouldhop (Goldehope, Goldhoppe),
    Clarissa, 79

    Robert, 4, 75, 79

Gower, Christina, 14

    John, 14, 17, 55

Grave, Thomas de la, 12

Gregory (Grigory), Stephen, 60, 73, 76

Greyston, Alice, 22

    John, 22, 28-9

guilds, general, xvi, xviii-xxi, xxx

    Guild of St Mary, Beverly (Yorkshire), xvii

    Guild of the Blessed Virgin, Swanage, xx

Gybbis, John, 75

Gylis (Gylys), Alice, 21

    John, 21

    Robert, 21


Halcumb, Roger de, 70

Halle, John, 43

Hamell, John, 10

Harman, Henry, xxxiii, 66

Harrys, Agnes, 62

    John, xxxix, 62, 81

    Sara, 81

Hasard, Adam, 72, 82-3

    Eleanor, 79

Joan, 72
John, 53-4, 86
Robard, 62
Robert, 66-7
Walter, 50-53
Hatter, John le, 52
Haynolfe, Elena, 33
John, 33
Hayvyle, Isabel, 14
Robert, 14
Hayward, John, 50-3
Helier, John (priest), xxxvi, xxxi, 21
Helyer (Helyare, Helier), Joan, 49
Walter, 22, 25
William, 32-8, 40, 42, 45, 79
hemp, xiii, xv
Hemyok, Joan, 3, 21
Henry, John, 78
Henton, William, 52
Herdely, John, 24
Hethman, William, 73
Hichecok, William, 50
Hicks, John (architect), xiii
Hodesfyld, William, 54
Holard, Thomas, 62
Hole, Robert, 70
Holyborn, Thomas, 62
Homan, Amota, 32
Christine, 78
Elizabeth, 79
Elsota, 32
John, xxxv, 32, 82-3
Ulsot, 81
Honubone, Hugh, 58
Honybone, William, 57
Hoper, John, 39-40, 56
Hore (Hoor, Hoore), Agnes, 3, 78
Alice, 33, 82
Edith, 72
Joan, 3, 12, 32, 61, 79
John, 3, 5-6, 12, 16, 34
Nicholas, 33, 37-40, 82, 84
Richard, 55, 69
Robert, 32, 34
William, 3, 5, 42, 72, 83
Howchyn, William, 33, 59-60
Howden (Hauden, Hoden, Hodyn,
    HoudenHoudon, Howdon, Howdyn,
    Howdyn), Edith, 3, 14, 42

Edward, 3, 5-11, 14-17, 42
Howse (House, Hows, Huse), Alice, 4, 42,
    49, 73, 81
William, xxxix, 4, 7-11, 42, 45-6, 49, 55,
    73, 76, 81
Hulle (Hill, Hills, Hylle), Agnes, 43
Joan, 48
John, xxxix, 33, 39, 43, 48, 56-61, 64-5,
    67-8, 81
Robert, 60, 85
husbandmen, xxxv, xxxvi, xxxix
Hux, Walter, 69
Hyde (Hude, Hyder), Alice, 78
Hugh, 78, 82-3
John, 21, 81
Margaret, 81
Hyderward, Walter, 11
Hylbronde, John, 60
Hyrdeley (Hyrdely), Alice, 21
John, 21, 23-5

Irlonde, John, 84
William, 84
Isaac, John, 66

Jakman, Harry, 62
James, John, 22
Martina, 22
Jane, Isabel, 22
Peter, 22
Jesop, Edward57
Jolet (Jelet), Roger, 62

Keche, Alice, 56
John, 4, 60
Richard, 86
William, 33, 38-9
Kent, John, 86
Kenyll, John, 62
Killing, Richard, 68-9
William, xxxiii, 69, 70
Kings Lynn (Norfolk), Fraternity at, xvi
Kirsey, Stephen, xxxiii
Knollyng, William, 60
Knyke, Richard, 59-60
Koc, William, 82
Krideton (Crediton), Henry of, xxxiii, 69
John de, 70
Kyrsey, Stephen, 66

Lamisham, Nicholas, 67
Lane, John, 32
    William, 14
Lang, John, 39
    Robert, 60
Langer, Robert, 58
Lankill, Robert, 21
Lannerans, Richard, 12
Larkepathe, William, 11
Larkestock, Alice de, xxxii, 11
    Adam dexxxii, 11
Latther, John, 61
Laurens, Richard, xiv, 53
Leche (Lech), John, 22, 25-6
    Robert, 4, 78, 84
Leege, John, 22, 26
Leland, John (antiquarian/traveller), xv
lights, see also Candles, torches, wax, 11-12,
    50-1, 73
Lokier, Joan, 62
Lomb, John, 50
London, Broad Street, 1
Long, John, 61
    Robert, 61
Longhe, John, 38
Lyamisse, Thomas, 64
Lyllyng, John, 33, 39, 59
Lyme Regis, xiv
    , 54-5
Lyte, Richard, 53

Maneryng (Mannyng), Andrew82
    Hugh, 54-5
    Margaret, 82
Mangerton, 82
Mankeswill (Mankeswell, Mankeswille,
    Mankeswyll, Mankeville, Mankeswill),
    Elena, 78, 88
    Emota, 4, 81
    Joan, 3
    John, 4, 6-8, 73, 75-6, 78, 81, 88
    Julia, 72
    Margery, 73
    Thomas, 3, 5-7, 14, 16-17, 56, 72, 75-6
March, William, 17
Marshall (Marchal, Marchall, Marchel,
    Marchell), Agnes, 3
    Joan, 3, 12, 21, 42, 85

    Margaret, 33
    Richard, 33, 38
    Walter, 74
    William, 3, 12, 16-17, 21, 24-5, 42, 73,
        75-6, 79, 81, 83
Mason, Agnes, 42
    Walter, 5-7, 16-17, 42-3
mass (masses), 52, 69-71, 80, 88-9
mass penny (mass money), 4, 14, 38, 56, 60,
    73, 85
Mate, John, 82, 84
    Matilda, 82
Mattersale, Avice, 79
    Robert, 79
Maulard, Mabel, xxxiii, 71
    Terric, 71
Maunsell, Agnes, 43
    John, 43
Mayyow (Mayu), Adam, 28
    Isabel, xxxiv, 22, 59-60
    John, xxx, 22, 27-9, 61
Melcombe Regis, xiv
memorial service, 70
mercers, 33, 43, 61
merchants, xiv, xxxiii, xxxv, xxxviii-xxxix,
    68-9, 72
Merche, Richard, 55
Mey, Joan, 78
    William, 78, 82-3
Milleward (Millewarde, Milword, Myllward,
    Mylwarde, Myllward, Myllewarde,
    Mylword), Joan, 4, 22, 81
    William, xl, 4, 12, 15-16, 22-4, 81
Molleyns (Molyne), Thomas, 57, 66
Morton (Mourton), William, 72, 74-5
Mountfort, Alice, 42
    William, 42-3
Moxsage, William, 66
Muchey, Richard, 68
Muntigu, Alice, 43
music, see also antiphonaries, choir and
    singing, xxxix, xl, xli, xliv, 1, 18, 29, 88
Mustard (Mostarde), John, 3, 12, 21

Newton (Neuton), Alice, 33, 42
    Joan, 32
    John, 32, 76
    Thomas, 33, 36, 42-4, 49
Nicholas, John, 79

Norys, Thomas, 66
Notting, John, 69
Nottingham (Notyngham ), Joan, 72
    John, 72
Nything (Nithing, Nything, Nythynge),
        Edith, 4, 22, 32, 42, 79
    John, 4, 8-11, 22, 32, 34-7, 42-3, 79, 81

oaths, 4, 14, 74, 80
oats, 50
occupations of Fraternity members, see
        also; butcher, carpenter, dyer, glover,
        husbandman,
fisherman, mercer, merchants, painter, rope
        making, xxxv-xxxvi
office for the dead, 4, 73
Offley, Alice, 21
    William, 21
Olyver (Oliver), Joan, 42, 48, 59, 62, 73, 81
    William, xx, xxxix, xl-xli, xliv, 1, 10, 45-8,
        58-9, 61-2, 67-8, 73, 76, 81, 85, 81, 85
Orcharde (Orchard), John, 67
    Richard, 33, 39, 54, 59-60, 64-5
    Thomas, 59-60
Ovyet (Ovyat, Oyet), Alice, 32
    Christiana, 32
    Florence, 73
    John, 6, 9, 32, 34-6, 73
    William, 32, 35

painter, 43
Palmer (Palmar), Edith, 42
    Gowse, 21
    Joan, 3, 32
    John, 3, 5-10, 32, 34-8, 40
parish clerk, 18
Parnham (Pernham, Pernam), Lettice, 3, 12,
        21, 79
    William, 3, 12, 15-16, 21, 79
Parrok (Parocke, Parok, Parrock, Parrocke,
        Parroke), Joan, 4, 21
    John, 4, 21-9
Parson, Edith, 42
    William, 42-5, 49
Parys, John, 54
Passager, John, 50-2
Pawe, John, 73, 83
    Margaret, 73
    William, 73

Payer, Elisha (Eliseo), 38
    John, 59-61
    Robert, 61
Payne, Florence, 82
    Walter, 82
Percey (Percy), Florence, 32
    Walter, 32-4
Perys (Peeris, Peers, Perie, Peyers, Piris,
        Pyers, Pyrs, Pyrys), Agnes, 33, 42, 49,
        82
    John, 6, 8-9, 33, 38, 42, 48-9, 67-8, 81-2
    Lucy, 32
    Nicholas, 32, 34, 83
    William, 32
Peverell, Christine, 84
    Gilbert, 83-4
    Matilda, 84
Pewterer (Peuterer), Alice, 60
    Trobert, 18
Phipps, Joan, 79
    Michell, 79
Pistor, Adam, 12
Pitman, Joan, 21
    John, 21
Poole, Fraternity at, xxi
Porstok, Elias de, 69
Porter (Portour), Alice, 33, 62, 82
    Thomas, 33, 39, 47-9, 58-9, 62
Portesham, Matilda, 21
    William, 21
Potelle (Potel, Potell), Alice, 4, 33, 42, 79
    William, 4, 29, 33, 42-3, 79
poverty/poor relief, xvii, xix, 15, 73, 80
Powerstock (Porstok), 68-9
Preder, William, 81
Prest, Peter, 11
priests, xiv, xviii-xix, xxi, xxxi, xxxv-xxxvi,
        xxxix, xliii-xliv, 40, 57, 73
Prikepeny, Nicholas, 70
Prior (Priour, Pryour), Agnes, 21
    Hugh, 60, 62
    Joan, 84
    John, 21, 61, 83-4
Prout, Christine, 42
    Dens, 3
    John, 3, 6, 42
Pymor, Alexander, 49
    Joan, 49

Quarel (Quarell), Robert, 72
    William, 11-12
Quynteyn (Quintayn, Quintayne, Quintyn,
        Quyntin, Quynteyne), Agnes, 3, 12
    Walter, 3, 5-6, 12, 15-16
Raffe (Raaf, Raff), Alice, 79
    Christine, 78
    Henry, 79, 84
    Joan, 84
    Willema, 78
    William, 83
Rakerayne (Rawkerayne, Rawcreme),
        William, 48, 54, 59-60, 65, 85
Ramesham, Adam, 12
    John de, 70
    Peter de, 70-2
    Richard (de), 12, 69-72
Raw, Henry, 83
Rebe, Edward, 11
rector, 18, 21, 54
relics, 70, 91
Rendall (Rendal, Rendell), Emma, 22
    John, 22, 27-9, 53, 58-61
rental, 50-5, 57, 59
rents, 11, 54, 68, 70
Richard, Joan, 62, 73
    John, 59
Robyns, Joan, 22
    John, 22
Roger, Thomas, 79, 83
    William, 14
Rokerys, William, 61
rope-making, xv, xxxv
Roper, Stephen, 36
Ros, William, 81
Rose, Stephen, 69, 71
Rothoni (Roþiny), Hugh de, 69
    Richard, 12
Row, Alice, 84
    William, 84
Rugge, John, 58, 60
Russell, Agnes, 22
    Nicholas, 22

Sadler (Sadeller, Sadeler), Isabel, 42
    John, 42
    Thomas, 62
salaries, of officers and priests, 40, 56-7
Salisbury, Cathedral, 18

Salmon, John, 66
Samford (Sampford, Sanford), John, 56-8,
        86
Saunder (Saunders, Saundres, Sawnder,
        Sawndrys, Sawnther), Christine, 3, 21,
        32
    Edward, 3, 6, 9, 42
    John, 61
    Margery, 3
    Walter, 3, 21, 23, 32, 72
Scarlet (Scarlett, Skarlet), Alice, 42, 49, 54,
        61
    Robert, xl, 10, 42, 45-6, 54
Schawe, Thomas, 3
Scherard, William, 78, 88
Scheter, William, 85
seals, 11-12, 50-4-5, 64-7, 69-72
servants, xxxv, 32-3, 62
Seymor, Richard, 11
sheep, 57, 62
Sheter, Alice, 43
    Thomas, 48
    William, 43, 47-8, 61
Shippe, John, prior of St John's Hospital,
        83
Shyberd (Skibard, Skyberd), John, 69, 71-2
    William, 69
Singing, see also choir and music, 73, 89, 91
Skynner (Skenner, Skinner, Skynnere), Alice,
        14, 21
    Nicholas, 81-3
    Steven, 62
    William, 14, 16, 21, 23-5, 72-5
Smert, Thomas, 61
Smyth, Walter, 82, 85
Snaw, John, 11
Snaward, Richard, 52
Spyney, Florence, 42
    John, xxxix, 48
Stalbridge, Isabel, 78, 81
    Robert, 83
Staldeford (Stoldeford), Adam de, 69-70
    Matilda de, xxxiii
stall, 68-9
Stanton, Thomas, 52
Stapelford, Roger de, 70
Stawman, Isabel, 78
    John, 78
Stephen, Isabel, 72

Sterre (Sterry), Joan, 62
  John, 12, 17, 33, 38-9, 61-2, 64, 73, 75-6,
    79, 81, 85
  Lucy, 12, 33, 79
Stevyns, Nicholas, xxxi, 59
Stewards, xviii, xxviii, xxxi, xxxiii, 39, 55-60-
  1, 64-7
Stikylpathe (Stykylpathe), William, 54, 85
Stocfot, Walter, 69, 70
Stockefysh (Stocfysh, Stockfysch, Stockfyssh,
    Stokfisch, Stokfysh), Agnes, 33, 43, 48,
  81
  John, 57-8
  Thomas, 33, 35-40, 43, 46-8, 54-5, 61-2,
    67-8, 79, 81
Stone, Edward atte 12
Stork (Storke), Edward, 60
  William, 82
Stourton, 64
Stowre (Stour), Isabel, 3
  Joan, 32
  Walter, 3, 5, 23
  William, 32, 34, 73
Stratton, Richard (alias Ferthyng), 52-3
Streven, John, 39
Strowbrigge (Strawbrygge, Stroubrigge),
    Robert, 54, 58, 60, 64-5
Stykelane, Katherine, 60
Styll, Christine, 3
  John, 3
Styrtyll, John, 3
Sule, Thomas de, xxxiii, 71
Swayn (Swayne), Christina, 33
  William, 33, 81-3
Syffirwast (Sifferwest, Siffirwast, Syferwast,
    Syffrawast, Syferweste), Walter, 34, 72-
  5, 83
Sylle (Syle), William, 58, 60
Symmys, Amisia, 14
  John, 62
  Thomas, 14, 17
Symondsbury, xliv
Symones, John, 72

Taillour, Edward, 50
tailor, 60
Tanner (Tannere), Alice, 79
  Idonia, 53
  Joan, 53

John, 50-3, 78, 84, 88
  Ralph, 79, 84
tapers, see also candles and torches, 88
Tapin, John, 70
Tayler (Taylor), Denis, xxxi, 56-8
  William, 53, 64, 86
Tengmowthe (Tangmoth, Tangmowthe,
    Tengmothe, Tengmouthe, Teymoth),
    Agnes, 82
  John, 39, 58, 60, 67-8, 82, 84-6
Thomas, William (chaplain), 42
Threder, Agnes, 21
  Richard, 21-3
  Walter, xli
  William, 23, 83
torches, see also candels, lights and
    fraternities, 22, 26, 29, 32, 36, 40
Touker (Tokere, Towker, Tuker), Elisota, 72
  Raynald, 62
  William, 24, 72, 74, 82
Tracy (Traci), Edward, 33, 60, 79-81
  John, 50-3
  Margaret, 33, 38, 79, 81
  Thomas, 65
  William, 50, 80
Trenchard, William, 66-7
Trowbryge (Trowbrygge), Richard, 54
  Robert, 61
Trowet, Alexander, 45-6, 79
Trygylty (Tregaltys, Trigylty, trycaldy,
    Trygalty), Agnes, 82
  John, 47, 61, 65, 67-8, 82, 85
tucker (towker), 81
Tyly, Richard, 61
  Robert, 60
Tynkelder, William, 84
Tyte (Tite), Alice, 3, 21, 32
  Edward, 53
  Henry, 3, 5, 21-2, 32, 34, 82-3

Vynsent, Alice, 81
  Ralph, 81

Wacle, John, 1
Wainwright, Thomas (antiquarian), xi, xxiv,
    xxix, 78
Walle, John, 72
  Katherine, 72
Walters (Walter), William, 14-16, 34

Walyse, William, 61

Warde, Robert, 48

    Walter, 22, 73, 75-6

wardens and wardenship, xx, xxiii, xxvi,
xxviii-xxxix, xliv, 4-12, 14-17, 22-9, 34-
40, 42-8, 50-2, 58,
60, 66-8, 71, 73-6, 81-2, 84-6, 88

Wareham, 18

Warner (Waryner), Joan, 43, 48

    John, 43

    Thomas, 48

Waryner, Thomas, 61

Waterman, Isabel, 22, 33

    John, 22, 33

Waudiz, John de, 69

wax, xvii, xix, xxix, xxxi, 4, 10, 14, 21-9, 32-
3, 38-40, 43, 45, 56, 70-1, 73-5, 80-1,
84-6, 88

Webbe, Eleanor, 4, 33

    Gregory, 73

    Joan, 14, 42, 73, 84

    Richard, 5, 7, 17, 42

    Stephen, 4, 6-7, 14, 17, 33-4, 36, 72, 75

Weer, Isabel, 33

Wever, Philip, 62

    Robert, 59-60

Wey (Weye), Joan, 43, 49, 82

    Thomas, 43, 46-9, 56, 82

Weymouth, xiv, xxi

wheat, 21, 50

Whor, Robert, 34

Whyte, Agnes, 4

    Christine, 4

    John, 4

Whytehorne (Whitehorn), Richard, 62, 86

Williames (Williams), John, 43, 45

Willyam, William, 82

wine, xxxi, xxxix, 56-8

Wodewale, Mabel, xxxix, 82

    William, 82, 84

Wyke (Wikes, Wykes, Wykys), Christiana, 33,
38

    William, 33, 38-9, 46-8

Wymarke, the widow, 21

Wyne, John, xxxi, 59

Wyppe (Wyp), Robert, 70-2

Yung, Joan, 4

    John, 60

    Nicholas, 4, 10